ZERO TO APEX

A BEGINNER'S CRASH COURSE IN TRACK DRIVING (WITHOUT THE CRASHING)

Zero to Apex
A Beginner's Crash Course in Track Driving
(without the crashing)

Published 2025 by Bigfoot Robot Books
http://BigfootRobotBooks.com

—————————

Auto racing is an inherently dangerous sport. The information discussed in this book is meant to supplement, not replace, practical training.

ISBN 9798999004000

51995>

9 798999 004000

This book is dedicated to JR, Mike, Eric, Jim, Jacques and, of course, Maggie, for joining me on the journey of racing, and for their years of support through my racing career.

ZERO TO APEX

A BEGINNER'S CRASH COURSE IN TRACK DRIVING
(WITHOUT THE CRASHING)

JOHN PARENTEAU

CONTENTS

INTRODUCTION

I got into racing later in my life, later than most people who hope to do more than a random track day now and then. I grew up with only my mother around, in a small town in Oregon, and while I was driving go karts on gravel roads from an early age, my mother had no idea how to find a more structured organization to help me really learn racing. And honestly, I had no idea how to look myself.

So it wasn't until I was about 30 that I met someone who suggested racing school. I didn't even know a thing like that existed! I had a good job and no responsibilities, so I decided to invest in racing for awhile, and I don't regret it one bit.

Racing and performance driving has always been a pure passion for me. I'm not mechanical or any kind of a gear head, I can't tear down an engine or describe how a transmission works, but the one thing I was always good at was understanding how a car responds on track. There's nothing like the feeling of being on the very edge of control, but knowing YOU are controlling it. One of my fondest memories is being in a pack of spec Miata's at Willow Springs Race Track in California, going through turn 9 at about 90 mph, a fairly low speed turn leading on to the front straight. As I was approaching the apex I remember looking around at the other cars, all dancing on the limit, but from my perspective as if in slow motion. I could SEE the subtle inputs of steering and throttle by each driver, using them to rotate the car tiny bits to optimize the exit. It was magical, and made me realize just how much an art racing can be.

This book isn't going to be the most technical manuscript about racing. If you are looking for something that really breaks down every term and mechanical detail of a race car and racing technique, there are many other books out there for that. What I wanted this book to be is a resource for first time drivers. When I started I had instructors and a program of racing that brought me up to speed. I know many track days, or HPDE (High Performance Driving Education) events you might sign up for have some limited instruction, but never enough, and always delivered at a moment when you are already overwhelmed by a wealth of new information, which makes it all hard to digest.

I wanted to provide a resource that you could study before you arrived on track, giving you a leg up, with key information you can put into action immediately. What I hope this book accomplishes is to give you enough background and concepts so that when you walk out there for your first session, you can speak the language of racing, and begin to build on this information with actual experience.

Racing is a blast, and if you take your time to understand the concepts here, you will learn to love it like I do.

QUICK TIP

While most of this book is focused on "Suspended Cars", meaning cars with suspensions (shock absorbers and springs for example), a lot of the concepts still apply to almost any form of racing, from motorcycles to karting. Weight shift is the big difference, and it is applied in different ways (or not applied much at all) based on the type of vehicle you are driving.

Be aware of that difference and the bulk of this book will still be valuable to you.

1.
WHAT'S SO SPECIAL ABOUT RACING?

D riving a race car can be one of the most exhilarating experiences you will ever have. Whether it be a Formula 1 car, a racing go-kart or your street car at an HPDE (High Performance Driving Education) event, the experience is very much the same, and the skills to drive the car are similar as well.

Most people who don't appreciate racing often have little understanding of the art of racing itself. To most, it appears as if the cars are simply driving around the track, with very little danger, exertion or risk involved. But the truth is that any level of racing is a grueling, physical and difficult sport. Wrestling a vehicle through turns at high speeds and at the limit takes incredible hand-to-eye coordination, timing, physical strength and conditioning. Top drivers are in as good shape as many marathon runners. In fact, some drivers use events such as the Boston or New York marathons as a form of training.

After you've spent some time driving at a somewhat competitive speed you will begin to understand why drivers are offended when people don't accept racing as a real sport. Until they've experienced it, even as a passenger, it's hard to grasp the physical and mental challenges faced, as well as the high level of concentration necessary to avoid mistakes.

When you're traveling at high speed, even a brief distraction, such as a dart of the eyes, can force a mistake. And in racing, even a minor mistake can have consequences, in lost time throughout the lap, or worse.

RACING IS ALL ABOUT PUSHING A CAR TO THE LIMITS OF ITS ABILITY TO STAY WITHIN THE BOUNDS OF THE TRACK

Much like a snow skier uses the edge of their skis to control the amount of slide across the snow, a race car driver does the same with a careful understanding of how **Friction**, **Weight Distribution** and **Power** affect the car. To make it through a turn as fast as possible, the car must be placed at the tires' limit of **Adhesion**, their ability to grip the surface the car moves across. Placed at this edge, the car slides across the track much like that skier on snow. But by being intimately aware of how the car is balanced, as well as the effect of power and weight on the car at any particular moment, a race car driver limits unnecessary slide, and moves through a course at the absolute edge of control.

While drift racing has developed into its own sport, it's important not to confuse racing as we are discussing, and drift racing. The skill of drifting is in literally <u>enhancing</u> slide, whereas driving a race car in a more traditional sense is the art of <u>minimizing</u> slide. There will still be some slide in racing, but it is more about trying to use only the very edge of the tires limits of gripping the surface. Excessive sliding in our type of racing causes you to lose speed, and often control, neither of which are desirable.

Imagine that skier, as they move through a slalom course. To avoid wasting time, the skier cuts each turn as tight as possible, and though they continue to slide across the snow, the amount of slide is carefully controlled. The difference with auto racing is that a mistake may result in much more dire consequences. A skier may simply tumble and slide to a stop (though at a competitive level, an error at such speeds might result in serious injury).

A race car, in losing control, may make harsh and brutal contact with a wall or another car. But a truly competitive driver places the car at the very edge of the tire adhesion and the track itself, flirting with danger to gain the greatest advantage over their competitor. As we continue, it will become much clearer how this is accomplished.

Is Racing Dangerous?

The simple answer is YES. Even at the beginner level, racing is still moving a very heavy piece of machinery around a track at a high speed. But it is only dangerous if you, the driver, don't learn the skills necessary to control the car, and the physics that are in play while on track.

When I raced in open wheel Formula-style single seaters they used to call me a very "technical" driver. I came to understand what they meant was that I was not very fast as I broke down the track in my head turn by turn, carefully processing how to approach each turn, and slowly built into speed over several sessions. By the end I was one of the fastest drivers because I had taken the time to learn the track.

It will be an early instinct, driven by your enthusiasm and "need for speed" to push the throttle pedal down and go fast. But that won't actually make you fast. Take the time to learn each turn, where to put the car, how to apply throttle and brake. This will give you the skills later to go fast, but in a more efficient and safe way.

In one series we had a young driver who was very fast in the fast turns, and very slow in the slow turns. It was clear he had the ability to keep his foot on the throttle in those fast turns by sheer bravery (or foolish ignorance), but when it came to the slow turns, which required a more technical understanding of how to race, he hadn't taken the time to learn, and thus didn't know how to drive the car quickly.

It's fun to go fast, but the assumption here, in reading this book, is that you want to learn how to actually drive properly. To do that, take the time to learn slowly. It will pay off in speed, knowledge and, most importantly, safety in the end.

Types of Vehicles

For the purposes of this book we are going to cover concepts that apply to one type of vehicle, but I wanted to take a moment to identify several types of racing vehicles that you might encounter. The tips and information in this book, as noted earlier, are focused on one type of car, but still apply to any of them, in differing degrees.

At the smallest physical level, but certainly not the most amateur is Karting. Unlike the go-karts you might find at most indoor amusement centers, or at theme parks, **Racing Karts** are quite different in their power and speed. But the biggest difference between a Kart and what we call a **Suspended Vehicle** is a Suspension (thus the name Suspended Vehicle). Karts have no suspension and thus do not respond to the same dynamics of **Weight Shift** during cornering. A Kart is a chassis directly connected to tires, and thus you don't have to be concerned with **Vehicle Dynamics** in the same way you would on a regular car.

Three are essentially two types of Racing Karts: **Sprint** and **Shifter**. The former have no gears, and use a centrifugal clutch system that responds to more throttle. Shifter Karts have linear gear boxes, much like motorcycles or modern race cars.

Suspended Vehicles have shock absorbers and coil springs, though the suspension also includes the tires, which are larger than Karting tires and contribute to the chassis flexibility. Essentially any street car, and most race cars are

Suspended Vehicles, and the majority of this book is focused on this style of car.

Finally, the other type we must highlight is **Manual Transmission** versus **Automatic Transmission**. As we discuss later in this book, racing is about car control in many aspects, one of which is how you apply gears, shifting, engine braking and controlling acceleration. These are things best done with a manual transmission.

An Automatic Transmission is designed for the public roads, where pressing the accelerator (gas pedal) down is your only responsibility to accelerate, and the car's systems choose which gear to be in at what **RPM** (revolutions per minute). This makes driving to the store easy, but doesn't provide the control we need on a race track.

It is possible to learn some of the concepts of racing in an Automatic Transmission, but it will never allow you to be fully in control of the vehicle.

An addendum to the Automatic Transmission discussion: Many modern "sports cars" have **Paddle Shifters** on the steering column, placed to the left and right just behind the steering wheel. These are designed to mimic the way higher end sports cars and race cars shift. In concept, the paddles replace the gear shift knob. But unless the car has a very high end transmission, or still includes a clutch, these Paddle Shifters are little more than an automatic transmission in disguise. They will not replace a true manual transmission.

2.
THE RACING LINE

In racing, going fast follows one simple rule; the quickest way between two points is a straight line. Though this basic concept goes a long way in describing the act of racing, there is far more complexity that needs to be considered.

First of all, there isn't just one turn, but a series of them. As you drive around the track, you have to consider not just how to take that one turn, but also how the exit of that turn may affect the entrance of the next.

The main point to be aware of is that there is a way to drive a race track that is the most optimum and efficient path for your car at your speed, which is called the

QUICK TIP

As you learn the line, always drive it when on track, even when first out warming up or cooling down from a session. It may feel silly to stay on the line when just going slowly, but the action of putting the car in the right place will become part of muscle memory. Also, taking the line slowly will let you analyze parts of the track you would not see at a higher speed.

Racing Line. But remember, the line changes as you drive faster, pushing your car more and more to its limits. It's important to treat the concept of the racing line as a fluid, ever changing guide, that is until you reach your optimum speed.

We could go on about the many details you have to consider to drive a course fast, and we will, but for now, let's focus on the basics of taking a turn, and the various terms that apply to the process.

BREAKING DOWN RACING TERMS

Racing Line - For every track and every type of car (as well as every experience level), there is a slightly different way to optimize the fastest path around each turn, and the track overall. This is called the racing line, or simply the **Line**. One of the very first things you will do at a new track (and also when revisiting old tracks) is to study the line to remind yourself about the aspects of the turn that are critical. Each turn has a specific place you start braking, where you turn into the turn, how much you turn in, and when you accelerate out of that turn in preparation for the next. This is the line, and is the first thing you must know about the track even before you get in your car.

In many programs the track officials offer an opportunity to take a **Track Walk**, which is just as it sounds, a walk around the track. But doing so enables you to look closely at landmarks, to study the conditions of each turn to help you understand them better. One of the best things to do on a track walk is to look backwards through a turn, helping you further understand the conditions you will soon take at a far greater speed, where you have much less time to see the track.

Always ask if it's possible to do a track walk prior to an open track session, or at the very least ask if an instructor can drive you slowly around the track for the same purpose. *Never simply go on a track without permission of the track officials.*

Threshold Braking - When driving a street car you rarely press your brake pedal down hard, to its limit, unless in an emergency. But in racing, this is how you slow the car down in the shortest amount of time, which is key to speed. You want to spend the least amount of time, and space, slowing the car as possible.

Threshold Braking is applying pressure to the brake pedal to the point where, if you were to press it even a little more, you would lock up the tires (stop them from rotating). Think about modern road cars and ABS, which stands for Anti-Lock Braking System. YOU become the ABS in racing, being able to slow the car as quickly as possible without locking the tires.

Only perform threshold braking in a straight line, before turn in.
Photo courtesy of Lindsay Grant/MassTuning TrackFest

Note that you only apply Threshold Braking in a straight line, before the **Turn In Point** (see below). If you are in a turn or start to turn the wheel while Threshold Braking, you will spin the car.

More on this later.

Trail Braking - While usually not encouraged in most race car training programs, trail braking is a very useful tool if applied correctly. While threshold braking is valuable for slowing the car prior to a turn, trail braking is a way to reduce speed as well, but also serves other purposes in turning the car (more on this later).

Simply put, trail braking is another art form using the break pedal. In this technique you maintain a slight amount of braking to continue to slow the car, but it is much more subtle than threshold braking, and you often apply trail braking during the turn. It's a technique to settle the car, help rotate the car through a turn more effectively, and avoid coasting through turns. It allows you to carrying more speed into the turn while **Scrubbing** (bleeding off) more speed prior to the **Apex**.

Throttle - Hit the gas! Punch it! Put the pedal to the metal! This one seems obvious, but how you use the throttle, or commonly called the *accelerator*, is equally important to how you use the brakes. In racing, you rarely slam on anything, and the throttle is included (along with braking). Rolling on the throttle helps maintain a balanced car and prevents loss of control. Similarly, lifting throttle can help turn the car as well.

Lifting - The term Lifting refers to coming off of the throttle, and is another key method to help turn the car. As you will see later in this book, racing is about balance and weight shift. How you brake or how you make it through turns at speed depends entirely on the balance of the car. Lifting affects that balance significantly. It simply means releasing some or all of the pressure on the accelerator.

Braking Zone - The straight segment of track just prior to your Turn In Point is called the Braking Zone. Ideally this area is as short as possible based on how much speed you carry toward the turn and how good your car can brake. A Formula 1 car can

QUICK TIP

A fast exit speed out of a turn is the key to good racing, rather than a fast entrance into a turn. Never compromise a good exit speed for a faster entrance. Simply put, better to go into a turn a little slower so you can exit fast.

brake from 200 miles per hour to a stop in 4 seconds, which generates an amazing 5 Gs of force on the driver.[1]

Turn In Point - As you might imagine, the turn in point is simply the point where you begin to turn into the corner. It may seem minor, but a turn in point can make or break not only your speed through the turn, but also your ability to take the turn at all. By finding the correct point to begin turning, you have set the car along a positive angle to accomplish the turn efficiently. Too late or too early, you will have to dramatically alter the cars angle and speed while still in the turn, an inefficient and sometimes dangerous mistake to make. The concept will make more sense further in this book.

Apex - While often mistakenly described as the middle of the turn, the apex is better described as the transition point between entering the turn and exiting it. Though describing the apex as simply the middle of the turn is sometimes true, it is better understood as the middle of *your* turn, in how you interpret the best way to take the corner.

When driving through a corner it is often advantageous to apex later or earlier in the turn, rather than the actual middle of the turn, to optimize your speed through and out of that corner. Rather than simply "the middle of the turn", think of it as the tipping point between braking and throttle, though even this is too simplistic, as you will see later.

Exit Point - Simply put, the point at which the car is no longer in the turn. Another key definition for the exit point is the point at which the turn you just took is no longer affecting the car with any lateral force. This just means you are now going straight, not in the turn, and able to accelerate down the track in preparation for the next turn. But the faster the **Exit Speed** you can carry, the faster you can continue down the straight to the next corner.

Note also that there are times when the exit point of one turn is actually the turn in for the next. Each turn and each track has its own unique challenges, which is what makes racing so much fun!

Oversteer - You might be more familiar with this term in its more casual name, the **Spin**. Oversteer is when there is more grip on the front tires and less on the back, typically during a turn. With the added grip, the back end of the car will slide around as the front end stays connected to the road. The car spins around the front end.

Understeer - This is also known a **Push**. Opposite to oversteer, this condition occurs typically when you carry too much speed in to a turn. As you turn the wheel, the vehicle is moving too fast for the front tires to grip, and the car pushes through the turn.

So let's break this down and apply these terms to an actual turn.

In Figure 1, you see a basic 90-degree turn. Look closely, this may be one of the few times you ever see one because you certainly rarely see them on the track! But for now, let's take a look. In this example we will be driving from the left side to the right.

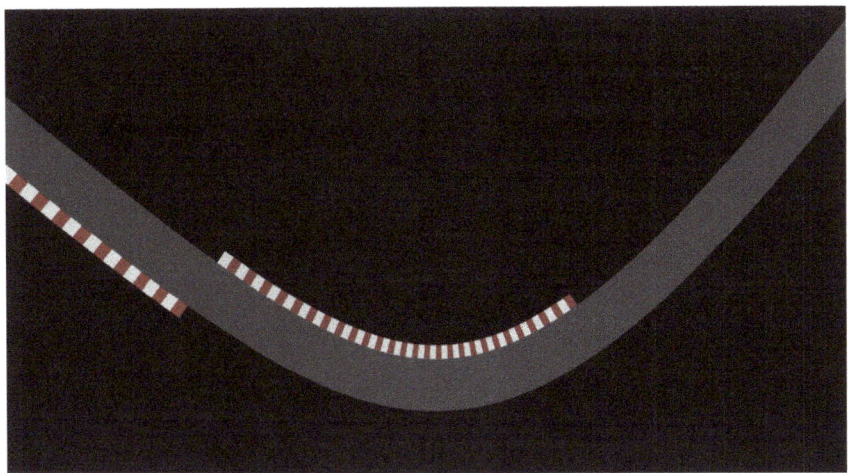

Figure 1

The driver slows the car as necessary in a *straight line*, on the far right side of the track, before the **Turn In Point**, then turns the wheel enough to just brush the inside of the track in the middle of the corner (the **Apex**).

The driver will then slowly **Unwind the Wheel**, allowing the car to move to the opposite side of the track, to the **Exit Point**, where the car is now moving down the track, straight once again. The goal through this is to take as much of the turn out of the sharp corner as possible, carry as much speed through the turn as you can without losing control or sliding, then exiting as you accelerate with as much speed as you can, building down the straight, or preparing for the next turn.

The Racing Line

Let's take a closer look at the Line of a turn. A quick reminder first:

Don't always listen to other drivers in other types of cars when they describe their "optimum line" through a turn. Depending on the type of car, the type of tires and a lot of other factors (including their level of experiences versus yours), the line will be different. It's important to slowly learn YOUR line through a turn.

 Also remember that the line might be described as the optimal path through a single turn, but when considering an entire track, it's important to remember that turns often effect each other. We'll talk about this later, but let's take this example from a basic level first, on a single turn.

Figure 1 shows an example of a 90 degree turn. Geometrically, the path through it, perhaps in a street car on a road, at a normal speed, is pretty much down the center of the surface. At normal "street" speeds there is no need to optimize the path because you are not navigating the turn for speed.

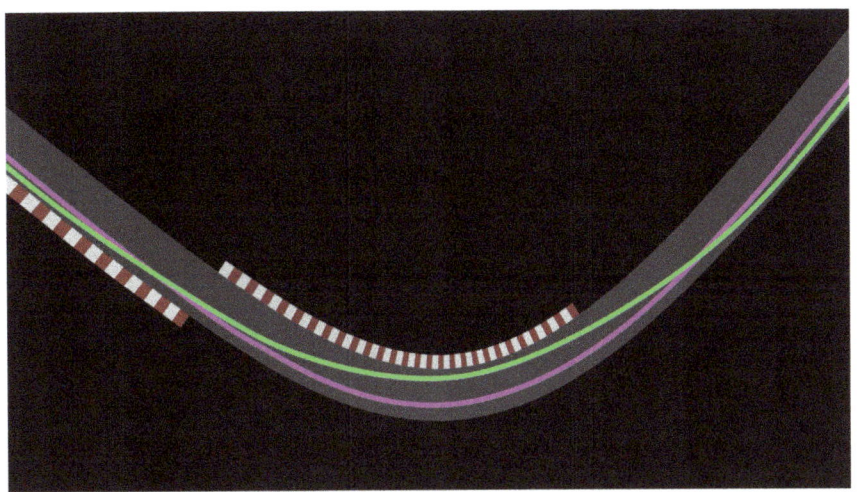

Figure 2

In Figure 2, a green line has been added to show a standard racing line, with the pink line the geometric path, or how you might take this corner in a street car at normal speeds. You can see how unlike the geometric pattern, the racing line flattens out toward the middle of the turn. The goal is to create as straight a line through the turn as possible, reducing the amount you need to slow down to take the turn.

The driver places the car to the far right side of the track (in this instance), then picks the turn In point that points the car toward the inner edge of the track, and the apex. As the car pushes past the apex the driver allows the wheel to unwind so that the car ends up once again on the far right side of the track.

While most turns are far more complex than this diagram, this is the basic concept of a turn, and how you will learn to breakdown your process of attacking them. Now, let's look at another type of turn.

In Figure 3, you see a corner that starts slowly, and then builds to a sharper turn at the end. This is commonly known as a **Late Apex** or **Diminishing Radius Turn**. In this case, you can see that the actual middle of the turn is somewhat behind

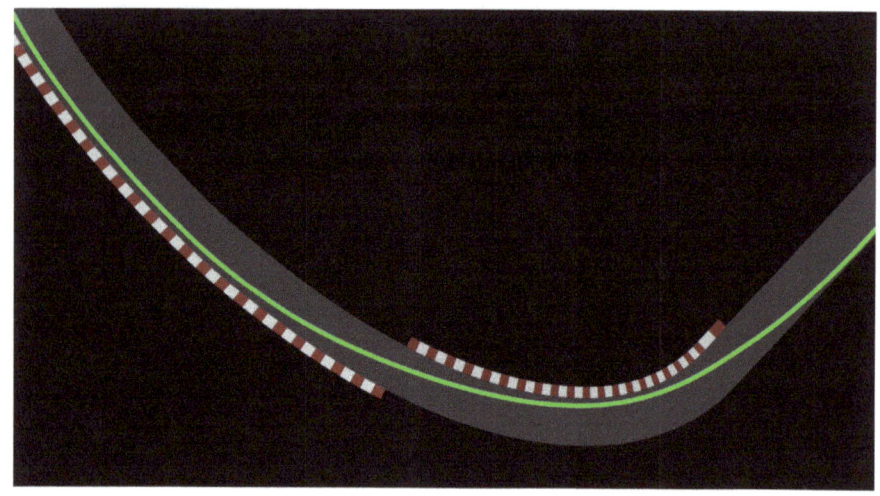

Figure 3

the apex shown here. The goal for the driver is to apply throttle at or before the apex, while still being able to complete the turn (on track, that is). If you were to apply throttle earlier, prior to the apex, you would carry too much speed through the turn, and then it would be necessary to lift, or release the throttle again, slowing the car a second time in order to complete the turn.

These are just two examples of turns with varying racing lines. Just as there are many race tracks there are even more turns, and with each turn comes a new line and approach. But the beauty of racing on a track for a day is that you get to take the same turn over and over again, slowly learning the best way to take it at speed. Repetition is the key to driving fast, just as learning how to precisely take each turn the same way each lap, which is harder than it sounds!

It's important to also understand that a racing line differs not only with each track but also with each type of car and each driver and their level of experience. Every car handles turns differently due to its weight, speed, braking ability, size and type of tires, and more factors. In addition, a driver just starting might take a different line than a very experienced driver at top speed. The lines may not vary greatly, but they will vary.

Also, as we discuss later on, no single turn stands alone on a track. For each line you choose through a turn, that line is affected by the turns before and after. While a straight away before and after a turn might make this detail seem irrelevant, most turns are in series, meaning the exit of one turn might be close to, or even THE entry to the next. Understanding how to set up for each turn best will inform how you take the turn before and after.

As you start driving on a track, expect your line to evolve from the first time out (even if you've studied the line on paper prior to driving) versus the end of the day when you've gained confidence and knowledge about how to drive. This is normal and part of both learning a track as well as learning yourself and your car.

3.

THE BUSINESS OF RACING

When teaching drivers, I often use the term *The Business of Racing*. What I means is, like any job, racing has steps that follow in a very specific order to ensure you accomplish a turn efficiently and quickly. While it is intense and fun to drive fast, to do it properly you will need to follow a specific formula.

As you approach every turn, the following five steps will always apply to some degree:

1. **Setup** - This is how you place the car in preparation for the turn. While in many instances you will position the car at

Figure 4

the far edge of the track opposite of the direction the turn will take you, this is not a rule. As mentioned above, you must take into account the previous turn, as well as the particulars of the turn itself, and the following turns to find the best placement. In Figure 4 we are assuming our basic 90 degree turn (which is a type of turn you might never see!) With an upcoming left turn. Thus the car is placed on the far right of the track.

2. **Braking Point** - Using the markers on the edge of track (which will be covered in a later chapter), you pick a consistent spot to start braking. Note that this is where threshold braking is applied. Your goal is to start braking as late as possible, and to slow the car to the optimal speed for this turn by the turn in point. This is an important note, that threshold braking must end, meaning you must be releasing the brake (no longer braking hard) by the next stage, the turn in point.

3. **Turn In** - At this point you release threshold braking and turn the wheel in towards the apex. The optimal goal here is to reduce your speed in the **Braking Zone** (the area between your braking point and your turn in) to enable you to rotate the car toward the apex without the need to brake more, or to apply throttle (because you slowed the car too much). During this time you might maintain some light braking (Trail Braking) as you approach the apex. Remember that the car is weighted heavily forward from the heavy braking (we discuss Weight Shift in a later chapter) and so too much braking, or sometimes even a little braking depending on your speed and the turn, could result in a spin. Also, if you carry too much speed into the

Figure 5

turn, the car will push past the apex, meaning the tires will not have enough grip to turn the car in the direction you prefer.

4. **Apex** - Ideally this is the transition from braking to throttle. Depending on the turn, you might simply be off the throttle or off the brake, or even at times only on a balanced or light throttle. But at the apex you will pick up the throttle, squeezing it on as you exit the turn. Remember to think of the apex not as the center of the turn, but as the transition point from entering the turn to exiting the turn. At the apex the car should be no longer trying to complete the turn in process, but rather be releasing the energy of the turn as you accelerate out. When we discuss weight shift this will become more clear.

5. **Exit** - Ideally you have squeezed on your throttle from the apex to the exit, ending up on the edge of the track. This is

Figure 6

the point where the lateral forces that effect the car no longer apply. The car is now *laterally balanced*, meaning the weight of the car is balanced left to right and no longer predominantly on one side.

Figure 7

As noted before, your exit may not always be the edge of track. If another turn is approaching shortly after this one, you might need to compromise your exit (and other parts of this turn) to take the following turn at an optimal speed.

To recap, following are the five stages of a turn:

1. **Setup** - positioning the car for the turn

2. **Braking Point** - The latest spot to begin threshold braking for the turn.

3. **Turn In** - The end of braking and the act of turning the wheel into the apex.

4. **Apex** - The transition point from entering the turn to exiting.

5. **Exit** - The end of the turn where the forces of the turn no longer apply to the car.

These steps, or modifications of them, will always be applied at every turn on track. As we will discuss later, there are complexities that affect the methods in which you apply them, but they always remain the same. Every turn has a setup, just as every turn has an exit. The type of turn, and how the car will react in that turn, will change depending on how these basic steps are applied.

4.

CAR CONTROL

W ithin the process of approaching a turn there is also a process of how to control the car itself through that turn. Everything you do as a driver is a critical element, from how you apply the brakes to how you grip the wheel. To start to understand this, let's define a few more terms.

Balance

There's no single word more important in racing than balance. Everything you do when driving affects the balance, and it is the balance that defines how well, or poorly, you navigate around the track.

Imagine your car, when standing still, is perfectly balanced on a point. With no external or internal forces on the car, the weight is equal on all four tires both front to back and left to right.

Every input you make, whether you accelerate, brake or turn, changes this balance. We'll dig into a lot of this later, but the concept of balance is the way understand how various forces change the efficiency of your vehicle moving around the track. As an example, if you navigate around a left hand turn, the weight of the car shifts to the right side of the car, the right tires. When you accelerate in a straight line, the weight shifts back to the rear tires, and equally lightening the load on the front tires.

While you can never keep your car balanced (and race at speed) on any track, how much, when and where you let this weight shift happen will define your speed through turns, as well as how you enter and exit them.

Braking Point

Determining your braking point for each turn is a critical element in building speed. As a beginner, the early task will be finding this magic spot where you feel you need to brake for a turn and, as you build speed and confidence, how you can push that point further and further toward the turn to minimize time off the throttle.

A braking point is often marked by a cone placed on the side of the track or sometimes a visual reference a driver chooses to mark the specific point to release the throttle and apply brakes. Remember in racing, for all intents and purposes, you are either on the throttle or on the brakes; *NO COASTING!* Coasting is lost time, and something that will add seconds to your lap time. As you learn any race course, you will become familiar with the braking points for every turn.

Though tracks often provide markers for drivers, such as the mentioned cones, these are not placed in any formal position, and thus are not hard and fast guides. Technically, cones are placed at specific distances, such as 100 feet apart, to guide the driver on the distance to the turn in point. But in truth, they are used only as guidelines, and if placed, are usually not measured for accuracy. This is fine since they are just guides, not rules, and it is up to the driver to discover their own best point of reference based on their ability and their analysis of the track.

A braking point is arbitrary and determined by your skill, your perception of the turn, your understanding of the limits of your car, and your bravery. The deeper you can brake, the longer you remain on the throttle. An experienced driver waits until the absolute last moment to brake.

Also, don't simply rely on cones. Sometimes the best marker to use is a crack in the pavement, a change in off track surface (from grass to gravel, for example) an access road edge or something that wouldn't normally be considered part of the racing surface. The marker is the one that YOU want to use to denote when you start threshold braking. Just make sure to pick something that is going to always be there. If you pick a discoloration in the road, make sure it isn't a shadow or some oil mark left on track, which will move or disappear over time.

As your skill increases, along with your understanding of the abilities of you and your car, you will find you are moving these points forward in space, making the spot at which you start braking closer to the actual turn in.

Revolutions Per Minute (RPM)

This may seem simplistic, but RPM plays a critical role in racing. As mentioned in the previous section, shifting quickly from a high gear to a low gear will suddenly increase the RPM in the motor, and equally as suddenly increase the torque on the **Contact Patch**, the part of the tire that touches the track surface. This rapid and disruptive action affects the careful balance of the car.

Beyond this, another concept that you will need to adapt to is the use of high RPMs. In a street car on the highway, we tend to keep our RPMs as low as possible. This increases gas mileage as well as wear and tear on various parts of the car. The only time we need some added RPM is when we are, for example, passing another car, or climbing a hill.

The **Power Band** of an internal combustion gasoline automobile engine typically starts at midrange engine speeds (around 4,000 RPM) where maximum torque is produced, and ends below the redline after reaching maximum power (above 5,000 RPM but less than 7,000 RPM).[4]

When on track it will be critical that you keep the RPMs in the power band, which will feel like you are over revving your car at first. But it is in that higher RPM where you will find your power, which is what you'll need to drive fast.

Down Shifting

When driving most of today's street cars we are often using automatic transmissions, so the act of shifting at all is done by the system, and we are barely aware of it. A race car is, by most definitions, a manual transmission car, which means you have to shift up and down gears yourself. We'll go into more of the reason a manual transmission is critical later, but for now let's talk about down shifting.

Down shifting is the act of changing gears from a higher to a lower gear; a fairly simple concept to grasp. The important point to understand is that shifting upsets the balance of the car. The idea of downshifting is to change into a lower gear ratio, reducing the output speed of the transmission and adding torque.

If you are driving on a road and are about to climb a steep hill, you might downshift to get more power to push the car up the hill. But remember, this will push up the RPMs of the engine. As you release the clutch in the new, lower gear, the car will often lurch from the sudden torque placed on the drive shaft since the car (unless slowed properly) will be transitioning, abruptly, from a lower RPM to a higher RPM. In a sense, it is like applying the brakes, but the sudden slowing is due to the difference in RPM between the transmission and engine.

If you wait until after your turn in point before you shift, and then you put the car into a lower gear, the car will become unsteady, making it much more likely you will lose control. If you remember the concept of balance above, downshifting AND turning unbalances the car even more, making it unstable in the turn. Down shifting customarily takes place at the end of threshold braking, while the car is still in a straight line, and when the all important braking period is nearly complete. That is critical to highlight.

Down shifting is done not at the start of braking, not as you turn in for the corner, but in a straight line prior to your turn in.

It is started and finished in the last segment of threshold braking, while the car is still pointed straight. This reduces the impact of the torque change to an area where it will have less detrimental impact on the balance of the car. There is also another way to minimize the negative effects of the downshift, such as **Heel and Toe.**

Heel and Toe

A transmission in a car is the medium that transmits power generated by the engine to the wheels via a mechanical system of gears and gear trains[2]. The higher the gear, the higher the speed but the lower the torque. In racing, and with your experience level, each type of car will have an optimal gear it should be in for each turn which provides the right amount of power and torque to push the car through the turn. If you are in too high a gear there won't be enough power to push the car through the turn.. If you are in too low of a gear, the engine itself will slow the car too much.

As you move around a track you will shift up to high gears down straight portions, and down shift for slow corners. The process of downshifting from a higher gear (and higher speed) to a lower gear is critical during your braking zone.

If you imagine, for example, you are racing down a straight, approaching a turn. Your engine is under acceleration and at 6000 RPM. As you find you need to slow for the turn, you also need to downshift to a lower gear to navigate the turn. As you begin to brake, you press in the clutch to make that change. The RPM will drop because you disengaged the transmission from the engine for a moment. When you release the clutch again, in your lower gear, the engine will need to rapidly speed up again to match the new gear, and the speed of the drive shaft. If you can imagine that the engine has gone from 6000 RPM in this example, down to idle (say 1000 RPM), and then, when the clutch is released again, back up to 7000 RPM as it speeds up to accommodate the lower gear. This will cause a jolt in the balance of the car, an abrupt shifting of weight and balance.

Any disruption like this is unacceptable in racing and the Heel and Toe method helps prevent this. The technique takes some practice.

First, place your right heel in front of the base of the accelerator, and rotate your ankle so the ball of your foot is on the brake pedal.

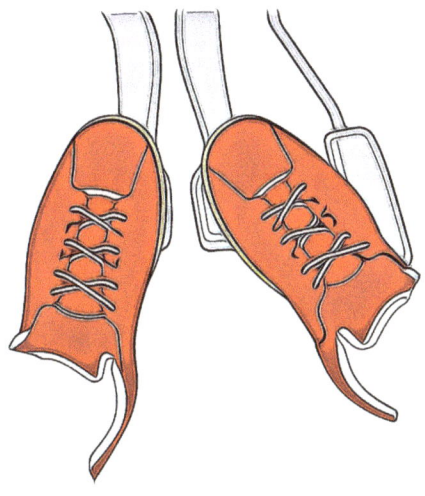

Figure 8

As you approach a turn you will be pressing down on the brake pedal. When you press the clutch in to shift, quickly roll your right foot over to the right so the side of your foot presses down on the accelerator briefly, releasing the clutch again as you do. The action is quick, just a brief press on the pedal each time the clutch is in (called a **Blip**).

By pressing the accelerator while the clutch is in you are keeping the RPMs of the engine up. Then, when you release the clutch, the RPMs of the engine will more closely match that of the drive shaft, thus preventing any disruption of the balance of the car.

You've probably heard race cars on track before, whether in person or on television. If you listen closely as the car is at the end of braking, you will hear this quick rev each time the driver moves down a gear.

Note that this is not something you can practice in your street car. In racing, your braking is much harder as you press the pedal down firmly and close to maximum (Threshold Braking). Because of this, the brake pedal is much lower, and closer to the level of the accelerator pedal, making Heel and Toe much easier to accomplish. On a regular street we rarely brake this hard, except in an emergency.

Unwind/Winding the Wheel

While it may not seem like it early on in your driving experience, racing is all about being smooth. Drivers will use terms such as "being smooth" or "squeezing on the throttle", which seem alien to a new driver going so fast on a track. Racing is a fast sport, but like anything, your mind will adapt, and something that seems too fast to accomplish will soon become much easier. Unwinding the Wheel is one of those concepts that seem strange, but are critical to racing.

CAN I LEARN TO RACE WITH AN AUTOMATIC TRANSMISSION?

Yes, but... as outlined throughout this book, racing is about being able to control the balance of your car. While learning the line is a critical component, and can be studied in any type of vehicle, what lacks in an automatic transmission is the ability to control the balance of the car. When shifting in a manual transmission, you can learn to manage every aspect of the car's dynamics, but an automatic vehicle prevents your ability to choose when to shift, how acceleration affects the car, the ability to manage your RPMs and more. So at a beginning level, while you can learn some of the basics, you will not be able to truly learn racing with an automatic transmission.

Figure 9

The term describes the process of slowly straightening the wheel back to the position it was in prior to entering the turn. Once straight, the car can proceed down the track with little or no friction placed on the wheels. Just as the turn in point is crucial, the process of unwinding the wheel is equally important.

At speed and in a turn, a sudden release of the wheel will cause the car to aim off track. To correct you will need to Wind the Wheel again, correcting your steering angle, which will cause a loss of speed and a disruption in the careful balance through the turn. Holding the wheel too tightly, and thus failing to unwind the wheel after the apex will upset the car, again requiring a reduction of throttle to avoid a spin. The goal is to point straight down the track at the completion of the turn, while using the maximum track possible.

Winding the wheel is the opposite, and a term not used as often, but is important to highlight. Just as Unwinding the Wheel as you exit a turn is important, turning in smoothly, or Winding the Wheel as you enter a turn, is just as critical. As we begin to discuss more concepts of balance this will become even more important.

Figure 10

Ten & Two/Nine & Three Hand Positions

Believe it or not, hand position on the steering wheel is also critical in racing. When you see someone driving down the street, often you see them with a single hand on the wheel, usually at the top. This is a horrible way to steer a car. In the event of any emergency, even something minor such as someone floating across a lane divider, you have so little control over the car to make quick and effective changes. Yes, its comfortable, and maybe you even think you look cool, but we quickly forget that we are controlling a (nominally) 3,000 pound piece of metal and plastic across a surface at speeds faster than normal humans can run. It should not be treated casually, whether off the track or on.

You hear of the typical hand position of **Ten & Two**, which places each hand halfway between the top and the side of the wheel. Ideally, the hands would be at the more traditional **Nine & Three**, which means they are halfway around the wheel from each other on either side.

There is more to this than just a conservative approach to safety. Driving on the public highways requires minimal effort, in most cases, to control a vehicle. Particularly with power steering today, there isn't much muscle needed to steer. But in racing, even with power steering, turning the wheel is more physical and more exacting. When driving around the track you need far more specific inputs into steering, whether that be rotating the wheel for a turn at the exact moment needed, or dodging a sudden slow car or other obstacle. If you were to race with the casual demeanor of the single hand driver, you would be unable to quickly manipulate the steering input correctly.

In addition, and as stated early on, driving a car at speed around a race track is physically challenging, and can be more so on your arms and shoulders from steering input. Maintaining a nine & three hand position will allow you to use less effort to turn the wheel.

The next time you are in your street car try and experiment. For a set of turns place your hands at nine & three and through each turn push the wheel with your outside hand as you turn. Don't make an effort with your inside hand. Let's say you are turning right. Push the wheel over with your left hand without any input from your right (Figure 10). Do this for a few turns.

Next, take another set of turns, but this time as you turn, pull down with your inside hand and don't use your outside hand. In the case of our right hand turn, this would mean pulling the wheel down with your right hand and just releasing your left hand from the wheel.

You will quickly get a sense that it takes far more effort in your arm and shoulder to *push* the wheel over the top rather than *pull* your inside hand down. While testing this driving around town might seem undramatic as an example, imagine these same steering inputs lap after lap, but with a level of necessary control that is the difference between staying on track or spinning.

Driving a car at speed on a track is not casual, requiring a lot of mental and physical effort, and you should do everything you can to minimize the stress on your body. Learning to use ten & two or nine & three even in your day to day driving as a practice will help you on the track, and in those unfortunate and hopefully rare emergency maneuvers in your every day life.

5.
VEHICLE BALANCE & WEIGHT SHIFT

To truly understand racing, it's important to grasp some of the dynamics that make a racing car tick. We deal with some of these things in our day-to-day driving, but racing enhances the importance of understanding them. First of all, remember that most race cars are rear wheel drive, meaning that the rear wheels are used for thrust, while the front wheels are used for steering. While this is not always the case, particularly if you are using your street car (many are front wheel drive, and sometimes they can be all wheel drive), the concept of how the car behaves is roughly the same.

Now, let's look at the concept of **Weight Shifting**.

Figure 11

Think of the car balanced carefully on a single point (Figure 11). While in a street car the optimum goal is to keep the car balanced, in racing we use the imbalance of the car at certain moments to increase our ability to take a course quickly and increase the vehicle's ability to turn. There are two types of imbalances: Front to Back and Side to Side.

Let's start with front to back Weight Shifting.

As a car accelerates, weight shifts to the back of the car. The suspension expands in front, shifting the weight of the car significantly to the rear suspension and tires, compressing them (Figure 12).

Figure 12

As a car brakes, the opposite happens, with the weight being placed on the front tires (Figure 13).

Now let's look at these concepts as placed on a race track. As a car speeds down the straightaway, the driver is typically on full throttle. The weight is shifted somewhat to the back of the car by the shift of momentum, but generally, down the straight, the car is balanced.

Figure 13

As the driver starts threshold braking in the braking zone, that weight shifts forward dramatically. With the weight of the car shifted to the front, the rear of the car is very light. If the driver were to turn the front wheels while under braking, the light back end would easily lose grip with the surface, pivoting on the heavy front end, spinning the car. This is why the majority

Figure 14 - Turning while a car is unbalanced might cause a spin.
Photo courtesy of Lindsay Grant/MassTuning TrackFest

of braking, and certainly any hard braking, must be accomplished while the car remains in a straight line. With the weight shifted forward, the front tires are compressed, which provides a larger **Footprint** or **Contact Patch**, the patch of rubber touching the road. This increases grip on the front tires as compared to that lighter back end and smaller contact patch of the **Unloaded** rear tires.

The driver finishes threshold braking, and releases the brake, starting the turn. With a higher percentage of the weight still on the front tires, this helps the car grip the surface and turn the vehicle. The front wheels grip better than the rear due to the increased contact patch, allowing the back end to pivot on the front. As the brake is fully released, the weight begins to shift back toward the middle of the car, providing more weight to the rear wheels and increasing the size of the rear tire contact patch.

As the car reaches the apex, the driver begins applying throttle. This shifts the weight further toward the back tires, increasing the size of the contact patch on the back tires while reducing the weight on the front tires. The added weight on the rear tires improves their grip, making the slowly

Figure 15

increasing power from the throttle effective in pushing the vehicle out of the turn. Steering begins to diminish however, as the front tires no longer have all the weight on them to fully grip the road. The driver begins to unwind the wheel slowly, reducing the turning input.

Now let's look at the *Side to Side Weight Shifting*.

As noted, the car is fairly balanced as it moves down a straight. Entering the braking zone, the car remains balanced left to right unless the driver inputs any turn to the steering wheel.

But as threshold braking ends and the driver begins to turn, weight begins to shift to one side of the vehicle, unloading the inside of the car as compared to the outside (Figure 15).

Depending on the angle of the turn, the car remains in a heavy imbalance through the turn and until the exit.

This is important to understand because your outer tires, the tires on the outside of the turn, are responsible for carrying the majority of the weight of the car now, and where they are placed is critical.

QUICK TIP

If racing in wet conditions, keep your outer tires off of any painted surfaces. While on a Dry Line, you might have your wheels on painted areas, these are often the most slippery areas when the track is wet, and are best to avoid.

Now, as we combine the actions of braking and acceleration with the side to side weight shift during a turn we can begin to see how balance is critical to maintaining control of a car but also optimizing its speed through the turn.

When we say balanced we don't mean, as in our car balanced on a single point, that the car must stay equally balanced at all times. What we mean is that controlling the weight shift of the car on that single point is the key to being quick. Losing control of how and when the tires are **Loaded** is when the car is no longer navigating turns efficiently, and will most certainly lead to losing control as well.

As the car experiences this weight shift we begin to experience a few new concepts. First, without getting too technical, it's important to understand the idea of **Slip Angle**. Basically put, the slip angle, which relates to your tires, is the amount your tire and its sidewall twist under turning, and more specifically, the difference between how much you turn the steering wheel and the rolling direction of the tire. The more slip angle the more **Cornering Force** is generated, which is the ability of the car to make the turn.

As an example, grab a pencil with an eraser and press the rubber end against a rough surface. Now twist the pencil and watch where the eraser makes contact with the surface. While the pencil twists, the rubber close to the surface twists at a slower rate, because the rubber touching the surface resists turning more than the pencil. This is slip angle.

Slip angle with regards to tires works the same way. With weight on a rubber tire, as you turn the steering wheel the rubber, which is in contact with the roadway surface, resists rotating because the patch of tire is sticking to the road. But further up the tire, toward the rim, the **Carcass** of the tire (the rubber that makes up the outer liner) flexes more as the wheel and steering mechanism urges it to turn. Street cars have typically very rigid sidewalls and have a low slip angle. Higher performance tires, such as racing slicks, have a higher slip angle, which helps the car navigate turns faster at higher speeds.

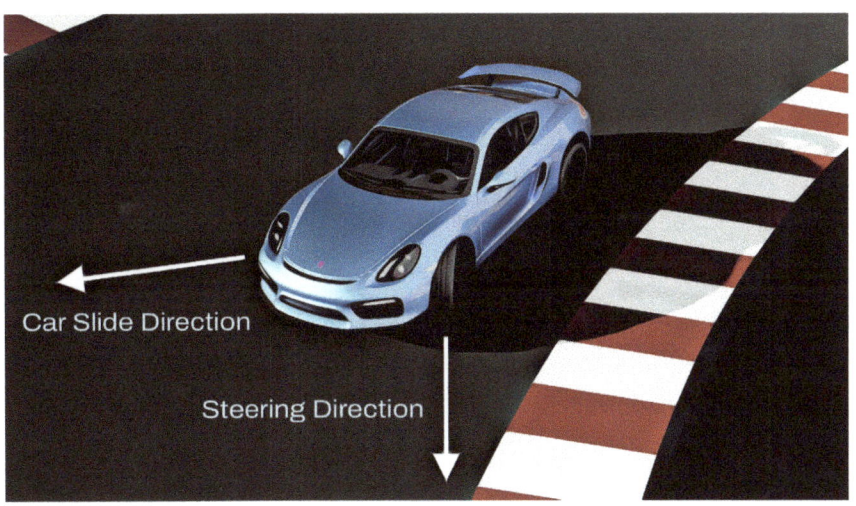

Car Slide Direction

Steering Direction

Figure 16

Simply put, the higher the slip angle, the more traction you will have.

All this talk of slip angle and weight shift add up to cornering force, which, as we mentioned, is the ability of the car to turn. Slip angle helps cornering force increase, up until you've reached your maximum grip, where the tire no longer helps the car turn.

How much weight is on the front end of the car when you turn, how much you turn, the type of surface you are driving on and the speed you are moving all add up to your ability to turn the car efficiently. When the car exceeds its cornering force, or when you turn the wheel and the vehicle no longer turns, you are in understeer, which means the car is no longer turning and instead going in a direction counter to the steering input. You might have heard the term **Pushing Through A Turn**, which is another way of saying you are in an understeer condition (Figure 16).

Imagine being on ice and turning the wheel. Because the surface is so slippery, it doesn't matter how much you turn the wheel, the vehicle just goes straight. This is what happens when you understeer, and is usually a component of too much speed and not enough slip angle or cornering force to make the tire grip the surface. While the ice analogy is an extreme, in a car understeer can be subtle, with only a small amount of **Push** through the turn, or larger amounts based on speed, cornering force and other factors.

Conversely, when you turn the wheel and the back end of the car rotates more quickly than it should, you are in an oversteer condition, also known as being **Loose**. This is caused by too much grip on the front of the vehicle, and not enough on the back tires.

Earlier we discussed the importance of completing your threshold braking in a straight line. If you were to continue braking hard and then turn the wheel, you would experience a very dramatic version of oversteer, or more commonly known as a spin. Spinning is the worse case scenario of having too much oversteer, and means you have lost control of the car.

6.
USING YOUR PEDALS

U p to this point we've covered a lot of terms and even got a little deep into vehicle dynamics, but now we need to apply this to your driving experience. As you begin to grow more comfortable with driving at speed on a track, you will begin to feel how the car is reacting at specific instances. This is the point where you will be able to start manipulating it to optimize the car's speed around the track.

As you move around the track you have a number of tools available to you to control the car. Of course you have the steering wheel that turns the front tires, but just as important is how you use the brakes, the accelerator (gas pedal) and the clutch. Let's take each separately to see how each can be used to go faster.

Brakes

Of course you use the brakes to stop the car, but how you use the brakes is critical to performance. The first application will be at the end of a straight section of track and before you reach a turn. We've already discussed threshold braking, which is the maximum application of the brakes before they lock up. Much like cornering force, the brakes have a limit as well, based on a few factors.

When we talk about brakes we are describing actually three components: Rotor, caliper and pad. The idea of a braking system is actually pretty basic. When the brake pedal is pressed, it clamps the pads in the caliper down on the rotor, slowing the car. Seems simple, which it is, but with performance driving we have to consider other factors.

As brake rotors are used heavily, they will heat up. If you've ever seen professional racing at night you will see the glowing red hot rotors when the car is under braking. This heat is caused by the friction between the brake pads and rotors. On a street car you never see this because even under the most wild street conditions the brakes are not used to this level. But in racing, the brakes are used often, and applied to the extreme, lap after lap, corner after corner.

There's not much you can do about hot brakes while on track, other than not use them, which isn't feasible if you are trying to optimize the car's performance. You can upgrade your braking system ahead of time, but that is another topic. The key point to understand is that like the rest of the car, and you as a driver, the brakes have limits. The more your car is closer to a standard

Figure 17 - Glowing brake rotors on an IndyCar
Photo courtesy of Chris Ortenburger/Flying Lap Media

street car (with no modifications, such as performance braking systems), the more of a concern this could be. When your brakes do overheat you will experience what is called **Brake Fade**. When you push on the brakes, they will no longer slow the car effectively. If you experience this on track it is time to pull into the pits and let them cool. Even a few minutes will make a big difference in their braking power.

QUICK TIP

When you return to the pits after a session, never hold the brake pedal down while you are stopped. The rotors are hot, and the pressure from the pads will warp your rotors. Once you reach your pit area, use tire chocks or the emergency brake instead.

Trail Braking
(warning, advanced technique!)

Beyond threshold braking there is another use for the brakes. Trail braking is an important yet often overlooked detail of racing dynamics. Imagine a race car as it moves around a track, with our car balanced on a single point. Under full throttle, the weight would swing to the back, tilting the nose of the car up. Under heavy braking it would swing forward, tilting the nose down.

Using these concepts provides a driver more tools for controlling the car than simply steering and throttle. Let's say, for example, that you are approaching a turn. Based on the rules covered so far, you would need to reduce your speed significantly to successfully make the corner. As you approach the turn under threshold braking, typically you release the brake at the turn in, before you turn the wheel, to avoid a spin. In this instance, however, you would not release the brake entirely, allowing a slight amount of braking to keep some weight at the front of the car. The result would make the front wheels stick to the track much better than the rear.

In a standard example, once you finish threshold braking, the brakes would be released and the weight would shift to a neutral front to back alignment. By keeping a slight brake application in, the car keeps some of the weight of braking on the front of the car. As you turn the wheel, the lighter back end will **Rotate** on the front tires with the larger contact patch, turning the car more effectively. The other benefit of trail braking is, once mastered, having the ability to carry more speed into the turn, which reduces the time for threshold braking. In Figure 18 we can see turn 2 at the famous Laguna Seca Raceway, Monterey, California (which is where I learned to race, incidentally).

Here, if you discard all of your speed prior to the turn (the braking zone on the left) then you waste too much time navigating the turn at a slow speed. Instead, using an

Figure 18 - Turn 2 at Laguna Seca Raceway
Photo courtesy of Chris Ortenburger/Flying Lap Media

effective application of trail braking as you enter the turn itself, shortens the braking zone while still ensuring the car reaches the correct speed at the apex.

Though this example is a good way to understand how weight shifting can help turn the car, it is important to understand two things:

First, sliding a car too much under any condition wastes time on track, overheats your tires and creates further problems in upcoming turns. A trail braking procedure to help turn the car should be carefully calculated to reduce the amount of time pivoting the back end, while still adjusting the angle of the car for the turn.

Second, the example should not only serve to understand how you can help turn the car, but also can be used as an example of how the balance of a car is a delicate and crucial factor in racing. If we go back to the introduction, and now examine what a layman's concept of racing is, we can see that no race car is ever just "driving around the track." Instead, the car is a constant ballet of power, braking and sliding to achieve an optimum goal. Add in the physical effort necessary for a driver to control a car under these conditions on a second by second basis, and an essence of the athleticism necessary to race becomes evident.

Back to Laguna Seca, turn 2. The practical approach to this turn would go like this:

Coming down the hill (on the left side of the Figure 18 image, coming toward camera), you threshold brake in a straight line for a shorter period than a standard turn, carrying more speed into the turn. As you reach your turn in point, you release 80% of the brake force, keeping 20% in as you turn the wheel. As you move into the turn you are scrubbing more speed off into the turn.

As you reach the apex, you have discarded all extra speed and have reached the speed needed to not only achieve the apex but also to accelerate out of the turn.

To complicate matters more, there is a third way to take this turn, also using trail braking. Rather than threshold braking to the far left side (as seen here), you line up the car to start on the left side but brake in a straight line past the first edge of the turn (the painted red and white curb), finishing your threshold braking in the middle of the turn instead. With this approach you then begin to turn the wheel at the same time you end your threshold braking. The delay causes the weight to remain mostly on the front tires, swinging the back end around until you are facing the apex and exit of the turn. Then, applying the throttle you "catch" the loose back end, push it back to the ground and power out of the corner.

As noted in the header to this section, these are advanced moves, and take years of practice to understand. I point them out only to show you just how many ways you can use braking, throttle and weight shift to move around the track.

Accelerator

Much like the application of brakes, the application of **Throttle** can effect the car within a turn. If we return once again to our car balanced on a single point we know that under acceleration the weight of the car shifts backwards. And, as we've discussed during braking, the weight shifts forward. While trail braking can work well to effectively rotate a car, so can the accelerator.

The basic rule of thumb for racing is no coasting. You should always be on some form of braking or throttle at all times. Coasting wastes time, which is the most important thing in racing: When a lap time comes down to a tenth of a second, even a slight coast could cost you.

With that said, as you enter a turn you might often find yourself too far from the apex, yet already in the turn, past your threshold braking and into a possible trail braking position. But just as a slight application of brakes can rotate the car by throwing the weight to the front end, a slight application of the throttle can do something similar.

In the introduction I spoke about an experience in a spec Miata at Willow Springs Race Park. This was a perfect example of using the throttle to rotate the car. In this instance the car was traveling at a high rate of speed (90-100 mph) but still IN the turn. No more brake application was needed to make the turn, and with the front straightaway following, losing any more speed would have seriously effected the upcoming straight-line speed. As the car reached for the apex, I was on a balanced throttle, which means the car was neither accelerating or slowing, but maintaining a neutral speed.

Figure 19 - A pack of Spec Miatas
Photo courtesy of Mike Woeller

With other cars around me, I had to carefully rotate the car to make the apex, but not lose speed. In this scenario I used the accelerator. With my balanced throttle, if I lifted off of the accelerator even a small amount, weight would shift slightly to the front tires and rotate the car in to the turn. Then, applying a slight bit of throttle would rotate it to the rear tires, giving them more traction while making the front push a little through the turn.

This is an advanced move, and only used when you as a driver have a strong sense of how your vehicle will react. But the example shows you the power of using the throttle to shift weight carefully in the car to affect change.

Clutch

While less effective in helping rotate the car, using the clutch and downshifting can help with managing your vehicle dynamics. As discussed before, when you approach a turn, all downshifting needs to happen before the turn in, but at the tail end of your threshold braking. Also, the use of heel & toe will greatly reduce the imbalance caused by the gear change, and the meshing of engine RPM to drive shaft RPM.

But knowing what gear to be in is critical to taking a turn effectively as well. Too low of a gear might be too slow, while too high a gear will limit your ability to accelerate out of the turn. The issue here is that every turn will be different for every car and every driver. Each car, and its combination of tires, brakes and suspension, will be able to take a turn at a different speed from the next vehicle. Similarly, your own experience, perception of speed and bravery will help dictate your **Cornering Speed** as well.

It can be a daunting task to take a car traveling at high speed and make it go through a sharp turn at the end of a straight. Considering the goal is to stay on the throttle until the last second, brake as hard as you can without locking up the tires, and then reach the optimum speed and gear BEFORE you turn in, it is a monumental task, and not one that is picked up quickly.

The best approach is the slow approach. Many more experienced drivers might tell you to use a certain gear, start braking at a certain cone on the side of the track, and to turn it at the last possible point, but remember, they are experienced, either on the track, in a performance car, or both. The best thing to do is take any tips under advisement, and then work your way up to your own choices, then build from there.

The key is to find the gear that feels right for the turn, that doesn't over rev your motor but also doesn't drop your RPM's too low. This can't be taught as much as experienced, but finding the right gear and getting to it before you turn in is a critical aspect to racing.

7.
SMOOTH IS FAST

Have you ever heard the term "smooth is fast"? In racing it's the idea that smooth, careful inputs are much more efficient than rough, jerky motions. It also applies to life: When you feel rushed, hurried or otherwise frazzled, you tend to make mistakes.

It's probably hard to imagine rushing down a straightaway at over 100 mph and understanding what it means to squeeze on the brake, rather than stab it. Similarly, in pressing the accelerator, turning the wheel, etc, all of that happens so fast on the track that it seems beyond reason to also ask you to be smooth with those inputs.

But as one of my instructors told me many years ago, the brain is an amazing tool, and will help you out in this situation. He used to say "the computer", meaning your brain, adapts to the speed if given time, and soon what seemed an impossible task of reacting on track suddenly becomes quite normal.

You ask almost any long time driver and they will tell you a story of a qualifying lap or hot lap where they were CERTAIN they were going slow, but it turned out to be their best lap. That is often because they got in tune with their vehicle, and weren't focusing on every little detail, but were instead one with the car, smoothly apply inputs almost instinctively.

Try this after you've learned the racing line on a track: Coming in to a turn, as you approach the braking point, lift your eyes up to the turn in point, then as you reach your turn in point, lift your eyes to the apex of the turn. Slowly become accustomed to your body knowing where to turn, where to brake, and allow your conscious self to look forward to the next actions you plan to take. By taking your mind off of each moment — in the moment — you will find that you are making less mistakes, and possibly going faster!

Driving In the Rain

This smooth input concept comes into play pretty heavily when racing in wet conditions. Any quick motions will often break the tenuous connection your rubber tires have with the damp and slippery racing surface. As rain hits the track, all the oils and dirt that have been dropped on the pavement by every other race car are quickly dredged back up, leaving the racing line in horrible shape for things like threshold braking or fast turn ins.

Figure 20 - Driving in the rain can be challenging.
Photo courtesy of Lindsay Grant/MassTuning TrackFest

Some describe racing in the rain as a drag race down the straights before you tip toe around the turns. That's not too far from the truth. The straights require little to no real lateral grip from the tires. So unless the rain is so hard that you hydroplane, which simply means there is so much water between the tire and the road that they are no longer in contact with each other, the straightways are not a major concern.

In a reasonably rainy session, the straights are where you will carry speed, but the turns are a different story. As mentioned above, the track becomes oily in the rain, and that oil comes up in the one place every other driver has driven, namely the racing line. Thus, it might be in your best interest to enter a turn off of the racing line, and avoid the Apex as well. These will keep you away from the worst parts of the track, and while your line will not be fast, it will help prevent you from spinning off track or even just sliding, which costs you time as well.

In addition, avoid any painted surfaces when the car is under load. Don't brake on a painted line even though that is where you brake in the dry. Slide off of that line just a little to avoid that slippery painted surface. Similarly, avoid apex and exit points that are painted. In any turn, it's a smart play to take a softer line, one that avoids the usual spots, if only to maintain a better level of traction through the turn.

Then floor it down the straight!

Well, don't floor it. Squeeze on the throttle. Smooth is fast, in the wet or dry. Learn to appreciate that and you will find you are far more in control of your car.

8.
THE RACE TRACK

Just like grains of sand (or snow flakes) every race track is different, No matter how similar turns might look from track to track, it's the little details that make them unique, and a fresh challenge to tackle. When I start driving a new track there is inevitably one turn that stumps me, but after awhile of trying and experimenting, I often find that turn becomes my favorite. Working to tackle a turn can be the most rewarding thing in racing.

Most tracks have some basic features which we can outline here, and are good to know before you venture to a racing event for the first time.

Pit Lane

This may seem obvious, but there are actually two types of pit lanes. First, the **Hot Pits** are what we all see on TV, the area where the car gets pit work done. Even within the hot pits there are two lanes. The outer lane, closest to the track, is essentially the pass through lane, like the fast lane on a highway, whereas the lane closest to the **Pit Boxes**, or the spots where you pull in to stop, is like the off ramp or on ramp.

When you enter the pits you start in the fast lane, and as you get closer to your pit box, or the person waving their arms telling you to stop where she/he stands, you move into the

55

closer lane, just before you move into the pit box area where the official is standing. The point of these two lanes is to avoid a conflict between cars who are slowing for a stop versus those speeding up to head back out on track.

Another aspect of the hot pits to understand the speed limit. Though not always posted, the rule of thumb is you take it slow in the pits. It is very unsafe to drive fast as you enter or exit the pits. There is not a standard pit speed limit that applies to all tracks, though a rule of thumb in my practice is keeping it around 20 mph at best. For events like HPDE you have to remember you aren't in a race so getting in and out of the pits fast is not critical. Take it slow and avoid any unwanted damages, injuries or reprimands.

Also remember, both for you and your friends who attend, the hot pits are considered part of the race track, so walking on them, particularly while the track is **Hot**, or active, is not permitted.

The **Cold Pits** is the area behind the hot pits, usually off the track where equipment is stored. It's usually cordoned off with cones or barriers, but is still considered part of the pits. The **Paddock** is the area where the cars stop for repairs or are just parking after a session. Similarly to the hot pits, and perhaps even more important, don't drive fast in the paddock. Unlike the hot pits, the paddock has many more pedestrians who are often unaware that vehicles are moving around them. Driving slowly in the paddock is a critical rule.

Blend Line

As you enter the pit lane from the track, or as you exit the pit lane back onto the track, you will often see a line that extends from the outside of the pit lane onto the track. This is called the **Blend Line**, and it is critical that you pay attention to it.

The idea of the blend line is to prevent slow moving cars coming back on track from interfering with fast moving cars.

Figure 21 - The blend line prevents slower traffic exiting the pits from entering the high speed line.
Photo courtesy of Chris Ortenburger/Flying Lap Media

Typically a pit lane exit is close to the first corner, and usually placed on the inside of the track. The racing line is usually on the opposite side of the track from the pit exit.

In our eagerness to hit the track fast, drivers usually want to dive onto the racing line as quickly as possible, but this can be very dangerous since your speed is much lower than racing speed, and by diving across the track from the pit exit to the racing line, you are in danger of creating a very horrible collision.

The blend line is a critical rule to follow. Typically it will force you to stay inside of the first turn, or at the very least, off the line until you have enough track space to get up to a reasonable race speed. Obey the blend line, both for your safety as well as others on track.

Braking Markers

Cones or number boards on track are used as markers to denote various things, though the most common use is as

Braking Markers. There are a lot of supposed rules about cones or boards, their distance apart and what they denote, but the one rule that will always hold true is that no track has the same markers as the next, so it's best to remember only one thing about them in braking zones: Use them for what you need them for, and ignore the rest.

As I approach a turn I use markers for two moments. First, I pick one to start my threshold braking, and then a pick another (often the last marker before the turn) as my turn in point. Sometimes the points I choose are halfway between markers, sometimes I ignore the official markers and use other markers on the track or near it.

There is no rule that says you have to use the markers, and sometimes they aren't reliable, with missing or misplaced cones, or a combination of cones and fixed number boards. The markers you choose will also change over time as you become more comfortable with a turn or feel you can brake later, for example. Use them as guides, and be willing to choose new markers as your confidence and experience grows.

Figure 22 - Number boards on the left or right of the track can be used as braking markers as well.
Photo courtesy of Lindsay Grant/MassTuning TrackFest

Figure 23 - Curbs can be high enough to disrupt your balance, which will affect your stability through a turn. *Photo courtesy of Chris Ortenburger/Flying Lap Media*

Curbs/Kerbs

The red and white painted surfaces, usually on the inside of a turn are called **Curbs** or in Europe **Kerbs**. They are usually some sort of cement or hard surface, and are areas you typically don't want to drive on. They are often raised, which will unsettle the car when driven over. There are times when the inside section might be flat, and can be used slightly more than their raised counterparts, but it is a good practice to avoid these until you are certain they won't negatively affect your balance.

Just note that some curbs are VERY raised, and sometimes high enough that you could high center your car, which might do significant damage to the underside. These high curbs are often found at the apex of a turn, which can be dangerous if driven over at speed, since at the apex the car is at the limit of balance during the turn, or most simply put, already on the edge of performance. Running over the high curb can push that careful balance over the edge, causing a spin. Until you are sure what type of curb is at each turn, it's best not to drive over them.

Rumble Strips

On the outside of turns, often in the braking zone, at turn in or on exit, you might also see red and white painted surfaces. These might be flat but also might be **Rumble Strips**, which are particularly evil-spirited surfaces designed to discourage you from driving on. They are usually sections of cement or other hard surface with ridges laid perpendicular to the racing line, which means when you roll over them they act like very small speed bumps. Optimizing the widest entry or exit is key to racing, and you might be tempted to use a little of the rumble strips to do so, but depending on the turn and the balance of the car, you might find using them disrupts the car too much in comparison to any advantage gained.

Run Off

Typically a **Run Off** area is an off track surface that provides an area for mistakes, such as an extra length of pavement past a straight before a sharp turn. If a driver fails to make the turn, the run off is there to let them go straight, rotate the car and return to track safely. It is also an area for cars to pull into if they have mechanical issues, to remove the car from the immediate track area, and thus from danger.

There is also another type of run off that you might see at the entry or exit of a turn. At a European race track called Snetterton, at the exit of turn 3, there is a section of surface that is placed outside of the flat curb. You might think it was an off track area, and illegal to use, but in truth is a legal part of the raceway. At times tracks decide to widen an exit to allow more room for the car to unwind to the edge of track,

Figure 24 - Using run off can lead to bad mistakes.
Photo courtesy of Lindsay Grant/MassTuning TrackFest

carry more speed and simply complete a turn safely. In the case of Snetterton turn 3, the added section lets you take more speed through the turn as the car pushes out to the edge of track and exit. It feels odd at times, and sometimes dangerous, to use these spots beyond the normal track, but make sure to check with track officials. Many times they are legal to use.

What does it mean if it isn't? If a run off area is designated as **Off Track**, it means it's not an official part of the racing surface, and is there only for safety. In a timed racing event you might have your lap time deleted for using it, or worse yet you might be disqualified. Often, in professional racing, even if the section of the track beyond the curb is paved and safe, crossing over into it is illegal.

Just as an example, at the famous Spa Francorchamps race track in Belgium, the famous high speed dual "turns" of Eau Rouge and Raidillon have significant run off at the exit. As you crest the hill of Raidillon you unwind to the outside of the track on the right.

Figure 25 - The exit of Raidillon has ample run off, but the area is not part of the legal racing surface.
Photo courtesy of Florent Gooden / Dppi/DPPI/LiveMedia

In the image above you can see the exit to the corner in the upper right of the image. The curb is clearly marked yet it is flat and there is significant pavement to the right of the curb. In this instance it is illegal to fully cross over this line into the track area to the right of the curb. This would be considered off track and thus illegal. The definition for Formula 1 and most other forms of racing is that you have to keep at least one tire on the racing surface. If you do so, you are still legally on the track (even though the majority of the car is over the curb.

It is these types of details you will need to learn for every track, for legality as well as safety.

Flag Stations/Corner Workers

While listed here last, this element of every track can be the most important, because it is these people who might save your life if you have a life threatening problem on track. The Corner Workers man strategic corners in protected areas that are visible to the driver. It is their responsibility to communicate with drivers on track using flags, which we will cover in the next chapter.

While it's easy to think of Corner Workers as watch dogs looking for you to make a mistake, in truth they are there for your safety, and will be the first and fastest way you will get assistance in an emergency.

It's good practice to make a habit on every out lap to spot the Corner Workers and Flag Stations so you have an idea of where they are located. Most importantly, make sure to pay attention to the flags they might be displaying to you throughout your session. These are critical signals to help you and protect you, and should not be dismissed.

I always make a point on my cool down lap to wave to the corner workers. They are volunteers (even at the level of Formula 1!) and are kind enough to come out to support you on your track day. And it doesn't hurt to make sure the people who might have to help you on track know that you appreciate them.

9.
ON TRACK COMMUNICATION

ommunication on track is an important aspect of racing. Within your vehicle you are limited in the ways you can communicate with the outside world, but the methods you can use are important for safety and showing your awareness.

Outside of the car, there are key players, such as Corner Workers at Flag Stations that can provide critical information about the track ahead, your own car's condition and your fellow drivers around you. Let's start by looking at Flags.

Figure 26 - *Photo courtesy Chris Ortenburger/Flying Lap Media*

Flags

Whether driving for Formula 1, NASCAR, karting or anywhere in between, **Flags** remain largely the same. The following group of flags are used at every track, and they all mean essentially the same thing.

Flags are designed to communicate critical information to you, the driver, while on track and it's important you know what they mean. Beyond knowing them its just as critical that you obey them. Remember, racing is a dangerous sport, and can be made even more dangerous if you treat the basic rules as cavalier suggestions instead of hard fast policy designed to protect you and everybody else.

Checkered Flag

In every driver's meeting you have you'll be asked to identify this flag. The fun answer is that it means you won! But in truth it simply means the session is over.

The important thing to remember is when you see this flag you should not continue at full speed for the rest of the lap. You should slow down, cool your car and your brakes, and even yourself.

The other thing to remember is that everybody else on track is going to be doing the same, so if for some reason you decide to continue at racing speed, you put yourself and those other cars in danger.

Yellow Flag

The Yellow Flag tells you that there is a danger on the track and should not be taken lightly. Typically a yellow flag tells you there was an accident ahead, and it's imperative to slow down. Even if a fellow driver decides they want to suddenly pass you, let them. You will be penalized if you don't obey yellow flags, including being banned from racing with that organization.

There are actually several ways that corner workers might display yellow flags, and each is important to understand.

First, a single stationary yellow flag means to slow down; no passing is allowed. On track days you are most likely attending, you will see all flag stations displaying this standing yellow as the cars for the session first enter track. This is typically displayed to note that this first lap is a warm up lap and no cars should pass or accelerate to full speed yet. You might also see this flag if there was an incident. The stationary flag might be displayed at all other stations, except the ones closest to the incident, to slow cars down and prohibit passing.

Often, at the start of a session, every flag station will display a single yellow flag, which tells all drivers to drive slowly and not to pass. This is typical for a driving event as cars are slowly released on to the track. Look for the Green Flag at the main flag station on the front straight before picking up speed.

A second way a yellow flag might be displayed is a Single Waving Yellow. This means you are about to come upon an incident and you must slow down. No passing is allowed. This waving yellow would be displayed at the flag station before the incident, and at the one at the incident, if there is one. You are not permitted to resume full speed or pass until you reach the next flag station that is not displaying a Yellow flag.

Finally, you might also see two waving yellow flags together. This is essentially the escalation of the single waving yellow flag, and denotes immediate danger in the area. You should slow even more and keep your eyes out for the incident, which might be on track or near it, and debris might be in your path. There also might be a tow truck or rescue vehicle on track. Keep your eyes open extra wide when you see a double yellow waved flag!

Red Flag

Red Flag is the sign of a major incident and the immediate need to stop cars from circulating around the track.

Depending on your pre-drive instruction, usually called a **Drivers Meeting**, a Red Flag can typically mean two things: Either to stop your car immediately on the side of the track, or proceed back to pits at a slow speed, with no passing.

If you are instructed to stop, pull over right away, but within view of a Flag Station. Don't pull off the racing surface but simply to the side. This will prevent you from getting yourself stuck if the off track portion is uneven or difficult to get out of, but will allow room on track for emergency vehicles to move past you safely.

Green Flag

A Green Flag signifies the start of a session. In a race this would mean cars can start racing, and is displayed at the main flag station at the Start/Finish line on the main straight away.

You might also see this flag after a full course Yellow to let drivers know the course is safe again.

In HPDE or timed events (as opposed to races), the green flag simply means the track is active and cars at now allowed to drive at speed.

Passing Flag

Getting passed at a track day should not be embarrassing. Considering you might have much less experience than other drivers, but equally as possible they might have a much more powerful car than you, or one that is race-prepared.. Learning to recognize passing opportunities, both to pass and to be passed, is an essential part of racing.

If a blue flag with a yellow stripe is displayed to you from a flag station, this means a faster car is approaching from behind, and they will want to pass you. Remember, unless you are actually racing for real, it isn't a badge of honor to refuse a pass or attempt to make a pass more complicated if someone is simply faster than you. It is best to accommodate the pass so you can focus back on the business of getting faster yourself.

What do you do when someone is going to pass you?

Almost nothing except lift off your throttle a little bit. <u>Stay On Line</u>, do not weave or put your car off line attempting to give the other driver room. The job of the car being passed is to stay on the racing line but to lift off the throttle enough to give the passing car the ability to pass more quickly. The passing car is responsible for going off line and around the car being passed.

The best thing you can do when you see the blue flag is at the next straight away to lift off the throttle rather than accelerate. Do not do this IN a turn. If you are about to approach a turn, stay in the braking zone and just slow the car early. The passing car will simply move around you and continue back on to the line.

If you ignore the blue flag or make it difficult for the passing car to get around you, you might see this next flag.

Black Flag

There are two ways you might see the Black Flag, either rolled up and pointed, or waving. The black flag means you did something wrong. In our previous example, if you have been ignoring blue flags and weaving, for example, as other, faster cars try to pass you, a corner worker or the main flag station might point a rolled up black flag at you.

This is a warning, telling you that the track officials are aware that you are driving in some unsafe manner. Sometimes a white board might be displayed with your car number on it to be clearer who it is intended for.

If you continue with the activity that caused the first pointed black flag, you might get a waving black flag. This means you must come in to the pits so that track officials can speak with you. It's best to obey these instructions or risk being banned from driving with the group again.

Don't think you can get tricky by ignoring a black flag. The corner workers and track Marshal communicate, so anything one official knows, the other's know as well.

A black flag displayed at all flag stations means the session has been suspended. In track day or HPDE events this typically means to proceed back to the pit lane for further instruction.

Meatball Flag

Though it has a funny name, this flag is important for the well being of you, your car and other drivers on track.

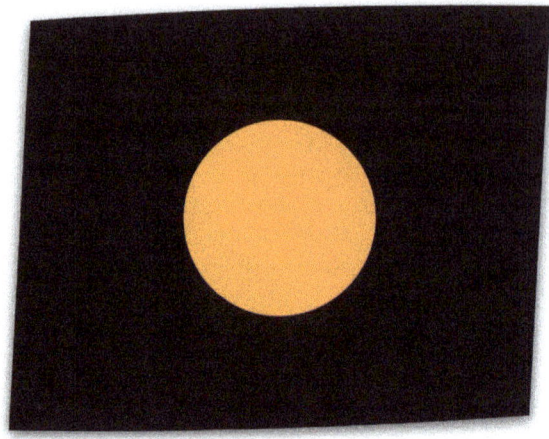

The Meatball Flag is signaling that there is something wrong with your car. This could mean a part is dangling or that you are depositing oil onto the track. Any of these reasons could be dangerous both for you and for other drivers.

Much like the black flag, you might see a white board with this flag to specify who it is intended for. It's important that you reduce speed and return to the pit lane safely.

Surface Flag

I know this as the Debris Flag, but this yellow and red striped flag means there is something on track ahead that could cause damage.

As in the previous meatball flag, if a driver in front of you drops debris or fluid, such as oil or radiator fluid, this could cause a dangerous situation for you. If you see this flag, drive with caution and try to identify where the debris is located.

If the debris is significant, or on the racing line, the course might turn to a full course yellow, with standing yellow flags at all flag stations and a waved flag at the station closest to the debris, so that a service vehicle can be dispatched to clean up the debris.

If the item or liquid is off line you might see a constant yellow flag displayed with this surface flag at the closest flag station for the duration of the session. Remember, if you see a yellow flag you cannot pass in that area.

White Flag

Though this is rarely used at track events, the White Flag means that there is a slow moving vehicle or an emergency vehicle on track.

Typically, at a track or HPDE event, before an emergency vehicle is dispatched on to track, the black or red flags are displayed at all stations, or the session is simply shown a checkered flag to end the session and return all cars to the pits.

Hand Signals

Flags are how the track workers communicate with you, but there are a few ways you can communicate with the drivers around you while you are in your vehicle.

Point By

When a car is faster than you there's not much you can do about it. The act of **Blocking**, which means weaving to keep your car in front of a car behind you, is illegal in most racing, and dangerous at the track event you will be attending. As noted above, if a car is faster than you its best to just accept it. If you're driving a Miata and they are driving a Porsche 911, they are simply going to be faster than you.

Figure 27 - A driver points to tell a faster driver behind which side to pass on, and that they are aware of the other car.
Photo courtesy of Lindsay Grant/MassTuning TrackFest

When you see a faster car approaching, or you are shown the passing flag, it's important that you stay on line, but you can also signal to the driver behind you that you see them, and can dictate how they should pass.

By sticking your left arm out of the window and pointing you can tell the approaching car that you want them and expect them to pass on the side you are pointing. If you are moving down a straight and the line is on the left side of the track, reach out and point over the top of your car to signal for the car to pass you on the right. If you are on line on the right side of the track, point straight out your window to the left.

A repeated, jabbing motion is customary. If for some reason you cannot effectively point over the top of your car, or your windows are closed, point inside the car so that the motion is visible through your rear window.

Fist Up

It's important to let drivers around you know your intentions, particularly if you are about to do something atypical of the normal racing process. One of these items is choosing to exit the race track to the pit lane. Unfortunately this signal is rarely encouraged, but is important to understand.

If you choose to head back to the pits at any time, as you approach the entry to the pit lane you would stick your hand out of your window with your fist raised. This signals to cars behind you that you are about to slow and exit the race track.

Why is this important? Imagine a car is closing on you and is ready to pass. If you were to simply veer off line toward the pit lane at the very moment the car behind chose to pass you, a collision could occur.

By signaling you are about to exit the race track, you let the drivers behind you know that they can stay on line. It is important that once you signal this intention that you move off line and reduce your speed. Also, do not change your mind after showing the signal and then veer back on to the racing line.

Other Hand Gestures

There are no other formal hand gestures that I have used regularly, though I'm sure you might experience others, formal or not. Despite the overwhelming feeling to do so, it's best not to display the middle finger when you did not like another driver's actions on track.

As noted above, one informal hand gesture is the wave. In addition to waving to corner workers on the cool down lap, waving to other drivers as you pass them, for example, tells them you are appreciative of their manners on track, just as they appreciate yours.

10.
GEAR FOR THE TRACK

<hr>

So you made it to the track, and with all the information discussed you are ready to put it into action! But there's a lot more to learn about a track day, whether testing for a big race series or simply taking out your sup'ed up street car for some hot laps.

First we should look at what you need to bring to have a successful track day. Some of these items might seem silly or unnecessary, but I promise you every one plays a role in your success throughout the day.

Helmet & Safety Gear

You will always be required to wear a qualified helmet on track day. While you can often rent these from the people putting on the event, you should consider buying your own. Remember that the helmet is designed to protect your head, which we can all agree is probably the most important part of your body. Putting aside the idea of using a rented helmet (who else has had their sweaty head in that?), you want to own, if possible, your own safety gear because it's all about your safety first.

Helmets must be Snell rated, meaning they will need a sticker in them that looks like the image at the top of the next page.

Image courtesy of Snell Foundation, Inc.

Note that the two letters, "SA" denote a helmet for automobile use. You cannot use a helmet rated for motorcycles, which will have an "M" instead. Also, the helmet should carry the current rating. In this case the rating is 2020, which means the helmet is legal to use until 2025. Get the most current certification that is available, which updates every five years. Most groups will allow the current rating or the one previous if the helmet doesn't show any signifiant wear and tear, but check with your particular group to confirm this.

Not to overstate it (which I don't believe is possible) but the helmet is critical. First off, you want something that fits you well, so buying your own will ensure this.

Second, make sure to care for your helmet like, let's say, a baby. Don't drop it or bang it around. Care for it, keep it in its provided bag when not in use, and treat it with care. It is the thing that will protect your head in the event of an incident.

Also note that helmets are usually rated for one major hit, meaning if you were to get into an accident and the helmet (and your head) had a significant impact, the helmet should technically be replaced.

I point this out not because you should expect you will have frequent impacts while at a track day (ideally you have none... ever), but dropping or banging your helmet around is almost the same thing. If you were to drop your helmet onto the pavement accidentally, you are diminishing your helmet's ability to protect your head. Treat it with care. Simple as that.

While we're on your head, racing drivers also wear a balaclava. These are the hoods you see under a driver's helmet, like a winter face mask you might see that covers the entire face except the eyes, and even extends down over the neck. This is made of Nomex© or other fire retardant material. At the level of club racing or track days this isn't required, though if you rent a helmet it will be, and the track should offer cheap versions of them, called "head socks" to help keep the rental helmets cleaner (though these are most likely not fire resistant).

My attitude with racing is the safer the better, and if I'm wearing what real racers wear, then that just makes me smart and cool. So if you buy a helmet, think about buying a balaclava as well. I also point this out because you should size your helmet with the balaclava in mind, as it takes up some space and might affect your sizing.

While less critical for your safety, some additional equipment can be helpful when driving. Proper racing gloves will improve your ability to grip the wheel and prevent any skin irritation (including blisters). A proper glove will be made of Nomex© or other material which is essentially fire proof. While this might not seem important for a track day, it is best to buy an actual racing glove if you can, and those will be made of this or similar material.

Also, while this might not seem important at first glance, racing gloves are designed with seams on the outside to prevent any unnecessary pressure to the skin or joints on the inside. It's all part of cool racing science, and it works. But wearing some sort of glove is a good idea.

As noted earlier, an important part of driving is how you work the pedals of your vehicle, so a proper shoe is helpful as well. A real racing shoe is both safe and thin, made up of Nomex© material as well, which resists burning. You probably don't need the fire resistant portion (though it never hurts to have) but a thin shoe is key to driving. When I first started racing, I tried out wrestling shoes, which are tight fitting yet thin, and thus perfect for driving.

Food/Water

Unlike a big race day for Formula 1 or NASCAR, a track day may not have many services, so the more you bring for yourself, the better. This includes food and water. It might not seem like it on the surface but driving on track is tiring, so drinking plenty of water is key. Bring a few big bottles and a cooler if you like them chilled, which is great if its a hot day at the track.

Similarly, bringing a sandwich for lunch and/or energy bars, for example, will keep you energized throughout the day. Some tracks might have a snack stand or food truck, but I've seen many track events with no food at all. Better to be prepared, and also healthier, than the fried food that might be offered. You don't want an upset stomach while driving!

Also note that some drivers might drive off track for lunch. I don't recommend this largely because tracks are often far from any restaurant or food source, which might mean missing a session. If you can bring food, it's the best way to stay immersed in your day at the track.

Tire Iron

While you rarely think about this in your day to day driving, you need to bring a method to tighten your tire lug nuts. Pushing your car around a track at speed will tend to loosen these lug nuts, and having a lug nut wrench or tire iron available, even if it's the one that comes with your spare tire, is wise.

Box or Large Bag

As we will talk about later, you will need to remove everything from the interior of your car, including your glove box and trunk.

You can prep for this at home by simply not bringing extra items and cleaning your car the day before the track day, but I've seen many a driver with a bunch of things they forgot which simply sits on the ground in a pile because they have no place to put it.

Bring along some sort of bag to keep your personal items gathered together and safe.

Painter's Tape

No track is perfectly clean, and with cars often venturing off track there is often debris brought back on, including small rocks. It's easy for a car in front of you to kick up these rocks and fling them at your car, breaking expensive items like your headlights, while also dinging your mirrors.

Painter's Tape or some sort of paper-based tape can be used to cover your headlights and any leading edges on your car. It might look silly, but the more seasoned drivers will be doing it.

Figure 28

Tires

While not always feasible, whether for space or money, you will see some of those seasoned drivers bringing a second set of tires to the track. Whether they are bringing a more race specific compound or simply don't want to burn up their every-day tires, this is something you can consider. Of course this also means you need to transport them, and unless you have a spouse or friend bring another larger vehicle, this might not be possible.

Also, another set of tires is expensive, and requires the addition of a car jack (something more robust than the one that comes with the spare tire) to make the process of changing your tires at the start and end of the day easier.

Make sure, however, that the spare tire you do carry is in good condition and has proper inflation. And if you are relying on the provided jack and tools for fixing your tire, that it is all in the car and working. It might be that you blow a tire, so it's best to be prepared, especially if you just drove your car to track on its own, without another vehicle accompanying you.

Personal Care Items

Track day can be hot, especially hanging out on the pavement of the paddock all day. Don't forget a hat and sun screen. I've seen many harsh burns on people who forgot that they would be spending a lot of time between sessions hanging out.

Figure 29 - A track day can be long and tiring. Bringing some comfort items will make it more pleasant.
Photo courtesy of Lindsay Grant/MassTuning TrackFest

Pop Up Canopy & Chairs

If you can swing it, bring along a pop up canopy or covering. As mentioned above, a good track day can be hot and sweaty, and you aren't going to want to sit in your car in between sessions. A small canopy and a few folding camp chairs will make the day so much more pleasant.

11.

YOUR DAY AT THE RACE TRACK

I t's finally here! You're going to your first track day. So what can you expect? Let's go over some likely elements you will face as you come to track.

Every organization is different and each might manage their track event differently. The first time you attend an event its best to ask about their process. It's critical to know how the day will work since track time is valuable and if you miss an important step you might find yourself sitting on the side lines instead of driving.

Following is a typical, at least in my experience, day with an HPDE track event. While some of these elements are not offered for every group, I'll outline them for reference.

Track Entry

If the event is being held at an official race track, which most are, there can often be an entry fee and paperwork to sign. As you drive into the race course grounds there will be a booth or gate. An attendant will usually be there to have you sign a waiver that says you are aware of the dangers of being on a race track and that you will follow the rules.

These waivers are both to help release the track of liability but also to make sure you act safely and responsibly when on their grounds.

Some tracks charge a fee as well, often $10 or so, though this may vary widely depending on the track. Carry cash with you for this to speed up the process.

Don't be shy about asking the gate attendant where the paddock is, the place where the event is taking place and where cars are parking. Tracks can be big and confusing if its your first time, and the gate officials are usually helpful.

Driving to the Paddock

Its exciting to find yourself on the race track grounds, and for once not as a spectator! But make sure to drive slowly while navigating around the grounds. And slowly means VERY slowly. This is not the regular street or a city neighborhood where the bounds of where cars drive and pedestrians walk is clearly defined. There will be a wide range of people and vehicles moving around, and it is very easy to get distracted.

Most track paddock areas have a speed limit in the 5 to 15 mph range. It might feel silly to drive that slowly but it is the smart thing to do. Also, you WILL get ejected from the track if track officials see you driving dangerous. So beware!

Paddock

Once you make it into the track you find your way to the staging area for the cars. Usually this looks like a very wide parking lot that is behind the pit lane. Parking spots are often long, as if for big trucks, because in some racing that is what they are used for, tractor trailer setups that are car transporters. In our world, however, you can use this larger space as your entire setup area.

Depending on the setup, there should be an area where the driver meetings will take place, the officials for the track organization putting on the event are based, and where your technical inspection will take place. Try to park somewhere close to these if possible. You'll waste less time walking to and from your car after each session if you do.

Fuel

Somewhere on the grounds will be a fueling station. Usually these are unmanned and provide both regular and high test/ high octane fuel. While this is a great backup, it's important you come to the track with a full tank already. The fuel at these pumps will be very expensive, and being unmanned are often flaky. I've been on track with people who have relied on these pumps, running their cars low before lunch, only to find their card wouldn't work at the pump and the closest gas station miles away.

Depending on how much fuel you burn, you might still find yourself low by lunch time, and will need a fill before the afternoon sessions.

QUICK TIP

At the track pumps you might see High Octane fuel offered. Make sure to read up on the value of high octane fuel and how it might affect your car. Not all street cars fair well with this type of fuel, and you might damage something as well.

Plan to get to the track early in the morning to spot the closest gas station to the track, or use the maps function on your smart phone to identify one, and how long it will take to get there. Then you can plan to run out at lunch to top the tank off. While running with less fuel means less weight, it's not a critical component to your learning process, and running out of fuel on track will be more embarrassing than it's worth.

Registration

As soon as you arrive on track you should find the are that is setup as the home base for the organization you signed up with. They will have a table where you will need to check in. Usually you are provided with a color coded wrist band, asked to sign any remaining paperwork, and are told your run group (more on this later).

The most important thing is to get the day schedule. Most driving groups stick to a pretty strict schedule for when your group gets on track. Nobody is going to wait for you when its your time to drive, and its your responsibility to have yourself and your car ready, and at the proper place, to take the track.

When you register, make sure to ask when the driver meeting will be, and where. This will be discussed later, but now is the time to find out where you need to be to start your day.

Inspection

A tech inspection is how the organizing group ensures that your car is track worthy. While daunting in concept, they are really just checking the basics. If your car is in fairly good working order, you won't have an issue.

You can prepare for the inspection before you leave home by simply emptying out your car of all the random junk we tend to keep in cars, which includes anything rattling around in the glove box and trunk as well. But the inspection is more than that. Most track groups require a vehicle inspection before you get on track, to ensure your car is in one piece and not a danger even before you roll out of the pits.

Before you leave home, check that your battery is secure, preferably locked down with straps or some mounting device. Check that you aren't leaking any oil, that your radiator is full and your tires are not too low on tread. Your vehicle can't have any loose or dangling parts. The idea of an inspection is to make sure your car is ready to be on track, and that nothing is going to fall off, drop off or scatter across the track for any reason.

Most events include a Tech Inspection Form. See below for an example. Most groups offer this form ahead of the track event so you know how to prepare your car, and often the forms are part of the self inspection phase, meaning they trust that you will check off these items yourself and provide the form to the track inspector.

Each group is different, but the same topics are covered. Make sure you request the tech inspection form from the group you plan to drive with ahead of time. Below is a sample from Mass Tuning in New England.

Note that while most forms appear to be self administered, someone at the track will check, whether officially with each car, or unofficially throughout the day, and if you did not prep your car correctly the organization can remove you from a session, or from the event.

Thank you for registering for MassTuning TrackFest. This is not a race but a day of educational, high performance driving. There are no timed laps or trophies. We simply have a focus on safety and fun in a legal road course. For this reason all vehicles must be maintained and meet the following guidelines. Making sure your car is track ready is your responsibility. Seek assistance if necessary.

Please fill this form completely and place under the wiper when ready to be inspected .

Year: _____ Make: _____ Model: _____ Color: _____

_____ DOT or Snell certified helmet, closed toe shoes and valid driver's license.

_____ Battery must be securely tied down with correct hardware.

_____ Brake lights must be fully operational.

_____ Brake pads and fluid should be track ready.

_____ Tires must be in good condition and inflated to proper air pressures.

_____ Lug nuts must all be present and have proper thread engagement.

_____ Steering and suspension components must exhibit no play.

_____ Fluids must be filled to minimum levels and not cause any dripping leaks.

_____ Engine belts and hoses must be in good, working condition.

_____ Seat belts or appropriate aftermarket harnesses must be secured correctly.

_____ Windows must be able to be lowered completely on both sides.

_____ All loose items must be removed from the trunk and interior including floor mats.

I, (PRINT CLEARLY) _____, agree that my car is in good mechanical condition and take full responsibility for the vehicle being driven on a closed road course. I understand this checklist is simply a list of minimum safety standards for driving on a track and that additional insurance can be purchased through motorsport providers such as Hagerty.

MassTuning does not accept any liability for the results of misconduct – everyone is personally responsible for any damages following their own judgment and waives all rights to lay claim resulting from any cause whatsoever either before, during or after this event.

Signature: _____ Date: _____

Driver Meeting

Prior to the start of the driving sessions there will be a mandatory meeting for all drivers. At this meeting the manager of the driving organization will discuss the schedule and any resources available to you at the track, including if any food services are available.

Second, the Racing Steward or Chief Instructor will talk about safety on track, provide a demonstration of the flags they will use during each session, and will emphasize safe practices on and off track.

While these meetings may seem frivolous, they are not. It's important to attend them and pay attention so you are clear on the rules of the day. Even Formula 1 drivers attend driver meetings, so at the very least you will be in good company.

This is also the time to ask any questions you have. Don't be afraid to ask even the most basic question. Anything involving safety is important, even if the more seasoned drivers act like they know it all. If it's about your safety, it's important.

Run Groups

When you check in to the event at Registration, you will most likely be told your Run Group. This is the way drivers are categorized largely by experience. Run Groups are not insults, but actually favors to you. If you are an advanced driver, the last thing you want to see on track with you is someone still learning the course or how to drive at speed.

But at the same time, if you are that first time driver, you want to be able to focus on learning the track rather than worrying about some fast guy zooming up behind you and forcing a pass when you aren't expecting it.

The best thing is to be in a lower, i.e. less experience run group to start and then, if you find you are comfortable on track, ask to move up to another group. This can happen if you can prove you are safe and have become comfortable at a more consistent track speed.

Ultimately, don't lie about your experience just because you feel embarrassed about being in a lower run group. You aren't doing yourself any favors, nor those other drivers on track with you. Be humble, and you will find the day much more pleasant.

Instruction

Depending on the organization, they will most likely offer some sort of instructions for first time or less experienced drivers. This could range from simply an experienced driver riding along with you, to a session by session instruction teaching you racing in a more in-depth fashion.

I began teaching in a very structured program, and I know it was truly valuable to drivers. Drivers in the beginning group would meet between sessions to go over specific areas of racing and then, during the session, put those into practice. While you have less free time to hang around the paddock, you learn far more, and are taught valuable techniques that ultimately make you a lot faster.

For most groups, however, they will offer an instructor to accompany you on track in the passenger seat. This is also called a Ride Along or Coaching. Ultimately, this person will have had extensive experience not only on that particular track but also in performance cars on track in general, and, if they are good, can teach you valuable skills that will last you a lifetime.

When you first sign up for the event at home you often have the opportunity to request an instructor. Some groups will ask you if it is your first time on this track, or if you are a beginner. Again, be honest. If you have driven on tracks before but don't know this particular track, you can request a Ride Along with an instructor for the first session.

But if you are entirely new, you should be assigned an instructor. The driver you will work with should know a lot about racing. Ask them what they've driven, what tracks and cars so you have an idea, but most likely they will have done a lot, and certainly more than you, which is what you want!

We'll talk about the basics of Racing School in a later chapter, but for now just be aware that the more you listen and apply what your instructor tells you, the sooner you will be running around the track at a safe and respectable speed, and the more fun you'll have.

The Sessions

Whether a beginner or more advanced, the rest of the day happens the same. If you remember at Registration you received your Run Group, which should have come with a schedule for the day. This has specific times when your session starts.

What is important to understand is two fold: The times are the START of your session, not when you should be getting in your car and getting ready. You paid for this day so it's important you pay attention to your session times so you are ready.

Second, there are no announcements. Nobody is going to tell you when it's time for you to get out there. If you forget, get distracted and miss your run group then you miss your run group. If you are late, you are just late, and get that much less track time.

So keep your schedule close to you, stay aware of the time, and as your run group time approaches, be ready in your car, helmet on.

You will need to know how to enter the Hot Pit lane where cars will line up for your Run Group. At least five minutes before your session is set to start, you will line up here. You might be asked to show your color coded wrist band (if that is applicable for the organization), to ensure you are with the right Run Group, and then you are sent off to merge on to track.

DO NOT speed in the Hot Pit lane, whether when rushing to join the back of the cue or when you are released on to track. Burning rubber when you are given the go ahead is a quick way to get thrown out of the track for the day.

Remember, as you leave the Hot Pit lane to merge on to track, stay off the racing line until you reach the first turn. If you recall our discussion of the Blend Line, which keeps the cars exiting the pit lane away from the racing line, it's important not to cross this line. If you are joining track after other cars, there is a chance they will be speeding down the straight and not ready to dodge a car just getting up to speed.

Your Day On Track

Whether a beginner or experienced driver, it's important to remember to check your car throughout the day. Watch your tire pressure, check your lug nuts after sessions and check with yourself as well, to make sure you don't have important questions or concerns. Ask someone with more experience if you do. This is not the time to be embarrassed if don't know something.

Racing at speed on any track is nothing to take lightly or casually. If you figure the average weight of a street car is around 2,800 pounds, that's a lot of weight you are throwing around at high speeds. Just make sure you take a breath, take your time to find speed, and don't take unnecessary chances, especially if you are driving home in the same car.

The art of racing is about finding the limits of yourself, your car and the track, but remember, this is just a track day, not a race. You don't need to get pole position or win a race. It is unlikely you will find yourself matched up against the exact same car with another driver with the exact same experience level, so comparing lap times is pointless. It's more important you have fun, learn the racing line, and understand what your car, and you, are capable of.

And hydrate. Lots of water. Very important.

12.
THE DETAILS MATTER

While we've touched on a lot of the bigger items in racing, from heel & toe through apex, hand positions and more, there are always other details that are equally important, but often over looked. They may seem silly, but if you pay attention to them it will improve your driving style over time.

Eyes Up

Imagine running down a sidewalk in a city. You decide you need to run around a corner ahead so you fix your eyes on the corner itself. As you approach the turn your eyes stay fixed on the corner without looking ahead. You keep your eyes on that corner until you pass the corner, and *then* you look up to where you are going next. If you aren't careful, by the time you look up you might run into something you didn't see ahead.

Racing is similar. While it's important to see the turn in point, for example, if you stare at the turn in point all the way until you reach the turn in point, you will be late in finding your next target, in this case the apex. At high speeds that delay in looking up is going to have a big impact on your efficiency through the turn.

Your brain and body are pretty remarkable in that they remember where things are around you, and can figure things out without you even realizing. In this instance, your brain after a few laps already knows where these racing markers are, even if you aren't sure. As you approach a turn and you see your first braking marker ahead, you don't have to stare at it until you reach it. Your brain sees it and is way ahead of you.

As you see that braking marker and begin braking, raise your eyes to the next item, in this case the turn in point. As you are almost at your turn in point, look up to the apex. Like in baseball, where an outfielder looks to where they want the ball to go (not at the ball itself) as they throw, your hands will follow your eyes and keep you on line, while your body remembers that you are just reaching your turn in point and knows to rotate your hands toward the apex.

And as you get close to the apex, raise your eyes up to the exit and trust your hands and head will still reach the apex.

Rest Your Hands

Even experienced drivers can discover they have a death grip on the wheel at times. Wrestling a car around a race track isn't easy and its likely you will grip the wheel too tightly through turns. Gripping too tightly reduces the ability to sense small changes in the movement of the car, which are transmitted through the tires to the steering wheel. It's important to avoid a tight grip, and keep a lighter touch as much as possible Remember to wiggle your fingers a bit as you move down a straight. Let the blood rush back into your hands for a moment.

We can take this into all areas of the lap as well. Soft hands, as its called in some sports, lets the motions and reactions of the car feed through your hands to your brain, and that input will make you a better driver.

Think of football. A receiver is taught to have soft hands, meaning to cushion the ball as it arrives like a shock absorber. If the receiver has stiff hands, the ball might bounce off their hands instead.

Similarly, if you maintain a lighter touch on the wheel you will be able to "catch" any actions of the car better, feeling when you might be loose or when the car is understeering, for example.

While driving super fast around turns might seem like a good time to grip the wheel, its important to find a balance on a firm grip but soft hands to improve your ability to sense the car better.

Breathe

Much like resting your hands, the straightaway is a good time to take a good breath and relax a bit. You might not realize that you were holding your breath, or just as possible, that you are breathing shallow. A few deep breaths every lap will keep you calm.

Studies have shown that deep breathing has not just immediate effects on your well being, but also long term effects on processing stressful situations. And what is more stressful than racing?

A key element to racing is staying calm. While this might be counter intuitive to what you are doing, the truth is, you can be calm and drive fast. As a matter of fact, being calm will make you faster!

As I mentioned earlier, one of my early instructors talked about "the computer" of your brain. It works much faster than our muscles and physical body, and when we get on track, often our body hasn't caught up to our computer. But once we become accustomed to speed it tends to feel downright normal.

Deep breathing (sometimes called diaphragmatic breathing) is a practice that enables more air to flow into your body and can help calm your nerves, reducing stress and anxiety. It can also help you improve your attention span and lower pain levels. [3]

Breathing is a big part of this. As we breathe we calm our nerves, take in oxygen for our brain to function better, and in a sense, slow the world down a bit. You will find that if you deep breathe a bit down the straights that the anxiety and tension of the pending turns will ease a bit, and that allows your "computer" brain to process what needs to be done better.

Scan

An airplane pilot is taught something called Visual Scanning, which is keeping an eye out though the windshield for other aircraft, while also scanning across the instrument panel.

For racing you should perform a similar practice. As you launch onto the straight, it's a good idea (in addition to resting your hands and breathing) to scan across your instruments. Check to make sure there aren't any warning signs or errors you should be concerned about. Check your fuel level.

A good pilot, whether in a plane or a race car, scans across from side view mirror, across the windshield to the opposite side, then across the instruments, to make sure all systems are go.

Stretching

Much like breathing, your muscles can also get tight and limit your ability to react to the car, or feel it effectively. Between sessions its important to get into the habit of doing some stretching. Even just touching your toes a few times will loosen your leg muscles a bit.

While it might not be believed in many circles, racing is an athletic sport. Professional drivers not only stretch but also adhere to serious workout schedules to strengthen muscles and maintain their flexibility. While you might not need to follow such an intensive program, paying attention to your body might be the difference between seconds on track, or even catching the car before you spin.

Before you go to track you should try stretching both your legs and back. In addition, stretch your arm out and lightly pull back on your fingers to stretch your wrists and forearm muscles.

In the Paddock between sessions, touch your toes, as mentioned, but also rotate your shoulders to stretch your back and consider some deep knee bends. All of this will increase the blood flow to your extremities and critical areas of your body. Like breathing, this will improve your reaction time on track, and your sense of calm in general.

13.
WHAT ABOUT RACING SCHOOL?

I often get asked if racing school is worth it. It's much like college in these modern days; you get out of it what you put into it. I went to racing school with the intention of trying to really race. While I only had partial delusions I might get paid to do so one day, I still wanted to take it seriously.

If you simply want to learn to race for fun, there are other ways to learn without the cost of a modern racing school. But again, like college, you get what you pay for. An introductory course at a racing school these days costs upwards of $5,000 for a three-day class, and that is just for the first level. Most schools offer advanced courses which teach more in-depth technique, and if you're serious you'll want to take every advanced course they offer.

When I began, I signed up for the first three-day course of racing school with Jim Russell Racing at Laguna Seca Raceway in Monterey, California. The scheduled event was still a couple months away so I went to Jim Hall Karting, a racing kart school in Ventura, California. I did their two one-day courses in kart racing as a way to prepare for the idea of racing in general.

By the time I got to the Jim Russell school I was comfortable with some basic ideas, and dove in to the three-day beginner's course. After that I signed up for the Advanced course as well. If you do well in the courses you can sign up for something called the Run Offs, which was a two-day event that had you lapping while being scrutinized by instructors. If you finished at the top you would get a free season of racing in their racing series (I finished third).

Despite not winning I still wanted to run in their series, so I paid for lapping days, or often called Test days, to further work on my skills.

At this point I haven't even raced in a real race, but the costs were already very high:

Jim Hall Kart Racing - Beginners	$600
Jim Hall Kart Racing- Advanced	$700
Jim Russell Three-Day Beginner's Course	$4,000
Jim Russell Three-Day Advanced Course	$5,000
Jim Russell Run Off	$2,500
Jim Russell Test Day	$1,500

So I've spent at this point around $14,300 to LEARN to race. From that point it gets expensive! And note that these are old prices. Assume anything similar these days is at least 20% more expensive, or more.

The upside of these programs is that you are immersed in the mentality of racing, and you are being taught by people who's sole focus is teaching you. If you have aspirations to really race as I did, or just have the money to spend, it's not a bad decision. Several of my classmates from Jim Russell did go on to race in NASCAR or IndyCar junior series, to name a few.

But for most of us who either want to just have fun, or are on a lot more limited budget, going to the right HPDE event could be the way to go.

As mentioned earlier, some track events offer much more than just an instructor in the seat with you. Even though they might charge a slight fee, an organization that offers a more in-depth form of training might do so for far less money.

I used to teach for a group called SpeedTrial USA in California. Beginners in the group would attend classes in between sessions where instructors would cover many of the same concepts that are covered in a full fledged racing school. It was impressive they offered all this for only slightly more than the standard fee for the track day.

So what really goes into a training program with an HPDE or track day? Let's break down some of the key elements you might find if you take part in a racing school program.

Class Time

While this may seem boring, spending time in class being taught the techniques of racing from an experienced driver can be key. It's difficult as a beginning driver to just jump in a car and drive. The concepts can be complex at first and when you are under the pressure of being on track, other cars speeding up behind you and more, it's hard to focus on technique.

Spending time in class to get the ideas in your head early will help, and when you get on track you can process the data more efficiently than with just an instructor yelling at you from the passenger seat.

May of the things you would learn in class are the same things taught in this book. But like any education, hearing different perspectives is valuable, so while this book is a great first step, finding additional class time will add, not detract, from your racing journey.

Side by Side

One exercise that can be very valuable to a new driver is an understanding of the spatial relationship between cars and your position on track. This can come simply in the classroom as well.

Often a lead instructor will have everybody stand up and stretch their arms out to their sides. While looking forward only, they will have you slowly move your hands to the front, calling out when you first see their fingers. You will be surprised at how well your peripheral vision works, and how far off to each side you can see without turning your head.

The exercise on track is a bit more real in that the lead instructor will line up cars side by side, and parade around the track in that formation. The goal is to stay close to the car beside you without looking that direction. While you will rarely (except at starts) drive in a formation like this, having a sense of how your peripheral vision works will prove valuable during a session. Also gaining some confidence that you can drive close to another car without actually hitting them, all without having to take your eyes off the track in front of you, is critical to building confidence.

Lead/Follow

In this technique an instructor drives a car, and you follow them, thus the name Lead/Follow. The idea here is that as the instructor places her/his car in positions on the track, essentially driving the racing line, you can observe and then duplicate their line.

An ideal session starts slowly, only focusing on the proper line. Then the pace picks up a little and you begin to observe where the instructor brakes, where they turn in for the turn, and how they accelerate out.

In a group setting it can be a bit more challenging, but typically all cars are lined up in a line and head out to track. The car immediately behind the instructor has the best view, and benefits the most. After a lap, usually on the front straight away, the instructor waves that first driver by and the next driver slots up behind the instructor for the next lap. The other driver can then move around the track, hopefully applying what they learned, and then join up at the back of the group.

As with anything, its the details that matter, and it's important the driver right behind the instructor pay close attention not only to the big signs but also the small ones. A good instructor might point out their window to cones or markers as they use them, or at their chosen apex, to make sure the student's behind see.

Figure 29 - Me in my early days at Jim Russell Racing

Corner Observation

At some point you simply need to drive. Most schools eventually reach a stage where they tell you to go and apply what you've learned in class, or in earlier sessions, to your own driving. Usually at this point instructors take a position at various key corners and observe, taking notes on how each driver navigates a turn.

While this can be nerve wracking if you pay too much attention to those eyes watching you, the goal here is to meet up with each instructor at the end and get notes. From the outside it's often easier to see mistakes, or even just points of improvement that you, as a driver, may not be able to see.

Is That All?

Well, yes. That's really the idea behind racing school. So you might ask why is it so expensive? For my journey I wanted to learn to race in Open Wheel, Formula-style cars and for that type of experience it gets expensive. If you've looked in to driving a super car around a race track you will notice it is usually a few hundred dollars just for a lap or two. When you are essentially leasing a car, and a real race car as well, it is not cheap.

Also, as noted before, racing school is a 100% focused class on racing. If you want to be immersed in it then this is how you do it. But if you are not expecting to ever race, even semi professionally, the expense may not be worth it. Sometimes getting good at driving your own sporty car around the local tracks is enough, and it doesn't mean you'll have less fun.

As with anything, it's all a matter of perspective, goals and the size of your wallet.

And Now, Off To the Track!

For many, racing becomes a life long obsession. I have certainly enjoyed pursuing it in any fashion I can for over nearly 30 years, and counting. Like anything, you rarely learn a skill and move on as an expert. Even professional drivers are constantly studying techniques to improve themselves. You might think instinct becomes the key to being fast, but in truth it is hard work to improve, and improvement in racing comes down to tens and hundredths of seconds.

I hope this book has given you some valuable information, and helped inspire you to pursue the art of racing. Whether as a fun hobby from time to time or if you want to find sponsors and start climbing the ladder, it all starts from here, the basics, which you will carry with you your entire racing career, whatever form it takes.

I'll leave you with a quote from my ultimate racing inspiration, Ayrton Senna, one of history's greatest race car drivers. He was a driver who not only drove with inspiration, but was a student of the art of racing, and took every opportunity to be better at his craft. As you learn to race you will begin to feel what he felt in this quote, if only a little. But that little bit is what will be the difference between you driving around a race track, and you being a race car driver.

Be safe out there, but have fun finding the edge. That's why you are here.

And so you touch this limit, something happens and you suddenly can go a little bit further. With your mind power, your determination, your instinct, and the experience as well, you can fly very high.

Ayrton Senna

ABOUT THE AUTHOR

John Parenteau is an accomplished filmmaker, writer, and performance driving instructor living in Southern California. He began driving on a tractor at the age of 10, when he was too small to push in the clutch pedal by himself, and has always loved driving almost anything ever since.

In addition to performance driving, John has driven and/or trained in almost every type of vehicle, from farming harvesters, and motorcycles to small airplanes and fire department apparatus.

Special Thanks to Chris Ortenburger of Flying Lap Media, Mike Woeller, Lindsay Grant of Life Essence Photography & Design and Armin from Mass Tuning for their generosity in providing images.

REFERENCES

1. Brian Silvestro. How Formula 1 Brakes Can Stop a Car Going 200 MPH in Four Seconds. APR 19, 2020. RoadandTrack.com

2. Sahaj Palla. Types of Car Transmissions – Different Types of Transmission in Cars. November 30, 2022. spinny.com

3. McKenna Princing. This Is Why Deep Breathing Makes You Feel so Chill. September 1, 2021. UWMedicine.org

4. Power Band, wikipedia.org

"Race Track - C .001 - 3.3km" (https://skfb.ly/osIPo) by Kristo.V is licensed under Creative Commons Attribution-NonCommercial (http://creativecommons.org/licenses/by-nc/4.0/).

GLOSSARY

ADHESION
The ability of a tire to grip the surface it moves across.

APEX
The transition point between entering the turn and exiting it.

AUTOMATIC TRANSMISSION
A vehicle device that manages the gear a car is in based on the vehicle's speed and the driver's application of throttle, and does not require any input from the driver to change gears.

BALANCE
The analysis of weight shift on a car while navigating a track.

BLACK FLAG
The black flag means you did something wrong. A rolled up and pointed black flag is a warning. A waved black flag requires you to enter the pits and speak with a track official.

BLEND LINE
A painted line that extends from the outside of the pit lane onto the track. It prevents slow moving traffic exiting the pit lane from moving on to the racing line. Crossing the blend line is not allowed.

BLIP
The act of quickly pressing and releasing the throttle. A blip is used during the Heel & Toe procedure.

BLOCKING
Blocking on track is usually defined as driving erratically in an effort to prevent a car behind you from passing.

BRAKE FADE
Overheated brakes that no longer provide proper stopping power.

BRAKING MARKERS
Cones and/or numbered placards on the edge of the track as you approach a turn.

BRAKING ZONE
Area prior to a turn used for straight line braking before the turn in.

CARCASS
The tire layer above the inner liner, which helps establish the tire's strength.

CHECKERED FLAG
A flag to denote the end of a session.

COLD PITS
Typically the area of the pits not actively used to service cars who are in a session. Cold pits might be behind a wall. A cold pit might also be defined as an area where no vehicles are racing or driving at speed.

CONTACT PATCH
The portion of a tire that is physically in touch with the racing surface.

CORNER WORKERS
Volunteer members of the race management staff who man corner stations, monitor track activity and use flags to warn drivers.

CORNERING FORCE
The lateral force produced by a tire during cornering.

CORNERING SPEED
The amount of speed taken into a corner. Cornering speed can also be defined as the amount of speed that can be taken through a turn in order to properly complete the turn as efficiently as possible.

CURBS
Segments of the track, typically found at the apex, entrance and exit of a turn, that help define the legal limits of the turn. Curbs are often painted red and white.

DIMINISHING RADIUS TURN
A turn that might appear to have a larger radius upon entry, but that tightens to a smaller radius throughout the turn.

DOWN SHIFTING
Transitioning from a higher gear to a lower gear.

DRIVERS MEETING
A meeting that occurs prior to any racing event where the track officials outline rules and necessary information to drivers and other track participants.

EXIT POINT
The point at which all cornering forces from the prior turn no longer affect the balance of the car. Also defined as the end of the turn.

EXIT SPEED
The speed of the vehicle at the exit point of the turn.

Flag Stations
Booths positioned at turns on a race track. Flag stations are manned by corner workers, who observe and monitor activity on track.

Footprint
Like Contact Patch, the portion of a tire that is physically in touch with the racing surface.

Friction
Friction is a force that resists the relative motion of two surfaces in contact.

Green Flag
A flag that denotes the track conditions are approved by driving at speed. You might see a green flag at the start of a session, or after a period of yellow flag activity.

Heel and Toe
The technique of braking while momentarily increasing RPMs to fascinate smoother downshifting.

Hot Pits
The portion of the pit lane where cars in the session actively enter and exit the pit. In professional racing, a hot pit is also where a car is serviced during an active session.

Kerbs
Segments of the track, typically found at the apex, entrance and exit of a turn, that help define the legal limits of the turn. Curbs are often painted red and white.

Late Apex
An apex not in the middle of a turn but rather later in the turn, toward the exit. A late apex is often seen in diminishing radius turns.

LIFTING
Removing pressure from the throttle pedal.

LINE
The optimal path around a race track. This various by type of car, the level of experience of the driver and the conditions of the track.

LOADED
When weight is placed upon a portion of the suspension through cornering or braking.

MANUAL TRANSMISSION
A vehicle device that requires a driver to place the car in a specific gear with the use of a clutch.

MEATBALL FLAG
A black flag with an orange ball that denotes a mechanical problem with your vehicle.

OFF TRACK
An area outside of the legal bounds of the racing surface.

OVERSTEER
When a vehicle's rear end rotates more than the steering input to the front tires.

PADDLE SHIFTERS
Modern system to change gears, located behind the steering wheel and operated by the left and right hands. Paddle shifters replace the gear shift knob in the center console.

PADDOCK
The area behind the pit lane where drivers maintain transport vehicles and park their vehicles when not on track.

Passing Flag
A blue and yellow striped flag that is waved at a slower car ahead of a faster car, to notify the slower car that they must allow a pass.

Pit Boxes
Marked spaces in the hot pit that define a vehicle stopping area. In organized racing a pit box is assigned to each team/car.

Pit Lane
An area parallel to the racing surface but separated by it, where cars can enter for service.

Power
In racing, power defines the amount of torque applied through application of the throttle, which provides acceleration.

Power Band
The range, defined in RPMs, in which an engine provides the most power.

Push
A loss of front tire adhesion, usually due to excessive speed. When pushing, the vehicle no longer moves in the direction of the steering wheel input.

Racing Karts
Open wheel, single seat racing vehicles with an open frame, no suspension and an exposed driver. Racing karts are available in both Sprint karts, without gear shifting, of Shifter karts, which have a sequential gearbox.

Racing Line

The optimal path around a race track. This various by type of car, the level of experience of the driver and the conditions of the track.

Red Flag

An emergency flag that denotes that all vehicles must stop on track immediately, or as defined in your driver's meeting, that all drivers should return to the pit lane. A red flag usually means a dire situation on track. Drivers should proceed slowly.

Rotate

The act of controlling the angle of the car within a turn using the subtle application of throttle and/or braking.

RPM

Revolutions per minute

Rumble Strips

Hard, grooved surfaces on the edge and/or apex of turns. The grooves run perpendicular to the travel direction, thus disrupting the car if driven over.

Run Off

An area outside of the legal bounds of the racing surface, often used as an emergency space for vehicles to avoid damage, or when a vehicle has a mechanical issue.

Scrubbing

Losing speed by allowing excessive friction. Also defined as the act of rubbing your tires against the surface by weaving at slow speeds, to remove debris.

Shifter

The handle used to shift the gears of a manual transmission vehicle.

Slip Angle
The difference between the direction a wheel is pointed and the direction the wheel is traveling.

Spin
Exceeding the ability of the rear tires from gripping the surface during a turn.

Surface Flag
A yellow and orange striped flag that denotes debris such as oil or fluids have been left on the racing surface. Proceed with caution.

Suspended Vehicle
A vehicle with suspension components, such as springs and shock absorbers.

Threshold Braking
Pressing the brake pedal firmly to the point just before the tires lock up and stop rotating.

Throttle
The method of controlling an engine by regulating the amount of fuel provided to the engine.

Track Walk
The process of walking the racing surface before any active sessions to better understand the racing line and track conditions.

Trail Braking
The application of smaller amounts of braking to reduce speed into a turn.

Turn In Point
The point at the beginning of a turn, in which you turn the steering wheel into the turn.

Understeer
A negative result of carrying too much speed into a turn. The vehicle does not react fully to steering input, instead pushing across the turn rather than navigating around it.

Unloaded
When weight is removed from a portion of the suspension through cornering or braking.

Unwind the Wheel
The act of rotating the wheel back to center position. Unwinding refers to the smooth process of rotation.

Unwinding the Wheel
The act of rotating the wheel as you enter a turn. Winding refers to the smooth process of rotation.

Vehicle Dynamics
The study of vehicle motion and the impact of changes brought on by weight distribution, thrust, braking, contact patch and more.

Weight Distribution
The placement of weight on a vehicle and its corners, particularly left to right and front to back, or a combination of these effects, which affect its ability to navigate corners on track.

Weight Shift
The movement of weight on a vehicle due to influences such as braking, acceleration and cornering.

White Flag

A flag that denotes a slow moving vehicle or emergency vehicle on track. It can also denote the final lap of a session.

Yellow Flag

A caution flag marking upcoming or current danger on a portion of the track. Standing yellow flags mean overall caution, while waving yellow flags denote a more immediate and present danger on track.

www.ingramcontent.com/pod-product-compliance
Lightning Source LLC
Chambersburg PA
CBHW051534120626
46551CB00012B/1220